Lightning Strike Press, LLC
14864 Birchwood Dr.
Spring Lake, MI 49456
P: 616-842-2814
E: Info@MindCaptureGroup.com

For information about special discounts for bulk book purchases, please contact Tony Rubleski at 616-638-3912 or via email: Tony@MindCaptureGroup.com.

Cover Designer: **Tonya Johnson** at Thoughts in Motion
Editor: **Asa Davis** at Second Look Communications
Interior Book Design: **Daniel Barrozo** at the Ink Studio

ISBN: 978-0-615-40202-4

**Proudly manufactured, typeset and printed by fine professionals who are all based in the United States of America**

# Advance Reviews

*Advance praise from top thought leaders for the third book in the bestselling Mind Capture business series*

*"Tony has nailed it with this book. In a busy, fast-paced world, a positive attitude and the right skills to match are essential for success as we head into the new decade. Mind Capture gives you the crucial tools to continue achieving higher and higher levels of success and prosperity-this is a must read!"*

**-Ivan Misner, NY Times Bestselling author**
**Founder of BNI and the Referral Institute**

*"Foundational or personal development training is critical to long-term success in business. If you build a house on a sandy foundation, it will eventually fall. Tony is now taking us on a course that shows us how to prepare our foundation. This is the book that makes his other books work even better."*

**-Kody Bateman, author "Promptings"**
**CEO and Founder of SendOutCards**

*"Tony Rubleski is Napoleon Hill and Norman Vincent Peale reincarnated! His genius, like theirs, has a solid foundation in the power of positive thinking coupled with intentional decision making. Tony does not consider "hope" an action plan, yet he delivers hope and empowers YOU to believe in yourself. Tony has followed his heart and it's a place that all of us should go. The truths that Tony uncovers are simple, but they do not imply an easy plan. Reprogram your mind. Wake up and understand that you control your own destiny. Tony's wisdom will result in an incredible journey if you will take the first step by reading his book and implementing change on a daily, consistent basis!"*

-**Sherri Lennarson, MAS**
**Immediate Past Chair of the Board – PPAI**
**(2010)**

*"Your most important tool for achieving success is your mind. Tony provides you with powerful insight that will help you push past your limiting beliefs and excuses to develop and maintain your personal success mindset."*

-**Tim Basa, VP of Sales and Marketing**
**www.nitelusa.com**

*"Finally! A book that encourages people to 'flex their marketing muscle' to achieve success!"*

-**Richard Fenton & Andrea Waltz**
**Courage Crafters, Inc.**

*"Outstanding, Amazing and Thought Provoking are just a few words to describe Mind Capture #3. The Book is a \*\*MUST READ\*\* for every entrepreneur who desires to create Explosive Results in their Lives. Tony, thanks for Your Relentless Commitment to Empower the world to Capture their Minds!"*

-**John Di Lemme**
**International Motivational Speaker**
**www.ChampionsLiveFree.com**

*"Tony reminds us that no matter what is going on around us in the world – in the economy, in the news – the cornerstone of success for anyone lies within one's own personal belief system. Anyone who owns a business or is considering starting one needs to put this book on the "must read" list next to Think and Grow Rich, and Rich Dad, Poor Dad."*

-**Dave Sheffield, Author and Entrepreneur**
**www.theshef.com**

*"Tony Rubleski is simply one of the best marketing and motivational minds on the planet! Read his book today and your business will soar."*

-**Patrick Snow, International Best-Selling**
**Author of Creating Your Own Destiny**

*"In this third installment in the "Mind Capture"series, Tony returns to his roots and reveals the #1 secret to why businesses are failing today and...More importantly he shows us how to shift our mindset, ignore the media and political naysayers, and become more proactive with proven ways to stay up in a down world. Brilliant!"*

-**Paul Guyon, Traverse City, MI**
**www.NonProfitFundraisingFormula.com**

*"Have you ever started reading a book and you could not put it down? Or if you did you could not wait to start reading the book again? Tony's newest Mind Capture book was a can't stop reading book for me. He definitely captured my mind. Tony is in a league all by himself concerning marketing techniques that really work. With this book, he has hit an inside the park home run! My only question after reading the book is when is the next one coming out?"*

**-Tim Green, President**
**Referral Institute of Michigan**

*"In today's challenging times, we all need every advantage we can get. Tony's latest book will give you the mindset to gain that advantage and competitive edge."*

**-Jim Packard, Distributor**
**SendOutCards**

*"Tony has done it again. His no-nonsense approach to business gives you a much needed wake-up call to make massive needed changes. Roll up your sleeves and get busy. Your Mind Capture future is waiting."*

**-Samantha Simon and Jolene Aubel**
**www.ShortCutConnections.com**

# About the Author

**T**ONY RUBLESKI IS CURRENTLY THE president of Mind Capture Group, based in Spring Lake, Michigan. He focuses on referral, retention and repeat marketing strategies. His second book in the series, MIND CAPTURE: How You Can Stand Out in the Age of Advertising Deficit Disorder (2008, Morgan James), went #1 in three different business categories on Amazon.com and received stunning reviews.

His core expertise, teaching and work focuses on the topic of 'Capturing' customers' minds. His work has been featured in various Radio and TV shows, Magazines and print and web-based newspaper outlets, from Bottom Line Magazine, The Detroit Free Press, the FOX TV network, Entrepreneur Magazine Radio, CNN Radio and NPR to the Inside Success Show. In March 2009, Northwest Airlines' in-flight magazine, *WorldTraveler*, featured **Mind Capture** as its Business Pages selection of the month.

As creator and editor of *A Captured Mind* newsletter, Tony has interviewed some of the highest-paid direct marketing, Internet, success and sales minds in the world including Seth Godin, Jay Abraham, Dr. Ivan Misner, Darren Hardy (SUCCESS Magazine), Jack Canfield, John Assaraf, Dan Kennedy, Bill Glazer, Joel Comm, Sharon Lechter and Larry Winget.

He's a 1994 graduate of Western Michigan University with a degree in marketing. In addition, he writes regularly and blogs for several national magazines on sales, marketing and motivational related topics. He's also a faculty member at the US Chamber of Commerce Institute program (IOM) where he teaches association and chamber executives marketing and technology related topics.

A highly sought after speaker and agent of change, Tony's live seminars and keynote talks continue to receive rave reviews from meeting planners coast to coast. He's shared the stage with business and sports notables like Les Brown, Michael Gerber, Bob Burg, Olympic gold medalist Dan Jansen and various celebrities including John Walsh, Mick Fleetwood and many others. He's presented to hundreds of audiences including some of the biggest chambers of commerce in North America, trade associations in the U.S. and private boot camps with attendee price tags of $2500.00+.

**Keynote & Seminar Topics Geared Specifically Toward Business, Non-Profit Groups and Associations:**

* *How to Capture & Awaken More Minds and Profits*
* *Exceptional MIND CAPTURE Customer Service*
* *Seven Trends To Help You Win In The Age of Advertising Deficit Disorder*
* *Referral Magic: How To Keep Your Customers Coming Back Again and Again*

> **WARNING:**  If You Have an Important Upcoming Expo, Annual Event, Conference or Breakfast/Luncheon Program, Get More Details On Tony's Speaking Programs TODAY!

FOR MORE INFORMATION:

E:  Tony@MindCaptureGroup.com

P:  616-638-3912

F:  616-844-0814

W: www.MindCaptureGroup.com

# OVER $100.00

## In Valuable FREE Mind Capture Bonuses Await you from Author Tony Rubleski:

1.   **Audio interviews with Ivan Misner, the founder of BNI, and success legend Jack Canfield ($100.00 value):**

   To access these two rare and valuable audio interviews conducted by #1 bestselling author Tony Rubleski visit:

   *www.MindCaptureGroup.com/bonus.php*

2.   **Free report titled, "350 of the Best Headlines Ever Written" ($20 value):**

   Send an email to Info@MindCaptureGroup.com with the subject line titled: 350 Report/Book Offer and we'll email you this valuable report that every marketing and sales professional should own and use to create strong marketing messages.

3.   **Free bi-weekly E-Letter and Facebook Updates:**

   Get 'Captured' with fresh updates, strategies and marketing resources designed to help you grow. Visit us today at *www.MindCaptureGroup.com* and click on the E-Letter subscriber box or join us at www.Facebook.com/trubleski

# MIND CAPTURE
How to Awaken Your Entrepreneurial Genius
in a Time of Great Economic Change!

# Table of Contents

# Foreword

**By Kody Bateman, CEO and Founder, SendOutCards,
and author of *Promptings: Your Inner Guide
to Making a Difference***

WE LIVE IN AN AGE OF information overload. As Tony would put it, it's a case of A.D.D. or Advertising Deficit Disorder. His Mind Capture series, which includes two best-selling books and highly acclaimed speeches and presentations, has addressed some of the best business building *"how-tos"* of this generation.

The book you are about to read will make it possible for you to take complete advantage of these *"how-tos."* If you have read Tony's first two books, you would know him as a business building expert — someone who can show you, step-by-step, how to dramatically improve sales and promote your business. What many of you may not know is that Tony is a great student of personal development. In this book, the student just became the teacher.

On these pages, you will discover that building a successful business is much like building a house. You must create a foundation before you can put up the walls and the roof. The foundation to your business is you. By nurturing yourself with personal development training, you strengthen the foundation upon which you will build the walls and the roof. The walls and the roof are what people see. In business it is the *"how-tos"* — the strategies and the step- by-step tactics to generating business. As we know, Tony is a master at training us on how to build the walls and the roof.

Here is the challenge: Most people want to skip the foundational training and jump straight to the *"how-tos."* This is the very reason that most people fail. Foundational or personal development training is critical to long-term success in business. If you build a house on a sandy foundation, it will eventually fall. Tony is now taking us on a course that shows us how to prepare our foundation. This is the book that makes his other books work even better.

I have become a great student of Tony Rubleski's training programs. He now provides us with the missing link: A call to take action — to quit simmering in indecision and negativity, and to become part of a new movement of positive action and constructive solution. He reminds us that now is the time to take positive control of your thoughts, to kick out fear and doubt, and let positivity propel you to the life you are meant to lead and share with the world.

# Dedication

*To my family for allowing me the chance to once again
share my knowledge, time and inner genius
with the world.*

# Introduction

IT WAS ANOTHER ONE OF THOSE, what I call, "thinking moments" on a flight from Chicago to LA, en route to perform a 'marketing exorcism' for a group of telecom executives. As I glanced out the window at the puffy white clouds below the plane's metallic wing to my right, my mind fixated on the question, *why do so many people continue to buy into all the fear-based talk and thinking running rampant throughout society?*

It's as if many people these days are walking around like zombies unaware of the power they possess. If only they snapped out of it and took a look at their life and where they REALLY want to go, and not where others or the media "think they should go." My mind searched for and delivered up several possible answers as to why people are so scared and operating from a fear-based position including:

- *The media is extremely good at message repetition – which lately has been nothing but negative*
- *People want job security – this is a myth which left the economic train station years ago*
- *The people they associate with are buying into all the fear – thus bringing them down*

- *They don't know what to do to block out negativity or how to design their mental space for good*
- *Most have never been exposed to personal development and positive role models, on a CONSISTENT basis, who support them and who see possibilities not road blocks*
- *Too many of them are waiting for their life to get better when they themselves should change it*
- *They choose to hide behind excuses and blame, versus seeking ways to positively change the situation for the better, even if it's painful at first*

## WHY THIS BOOK AT THIS MOMENT IN TIME?

After the first two books in the Mind Capture series, in which I shared specific ways to grow any enterprise via proven sales and marketing tactics, I'm returning to my roots. I have rediscovered the key ingredient most people are missing when it comes to building a successful business or organization: the power of a positive mindset. Some treat it lightly or as good old fashioned personal development. But to minimize and downplay its importance in today's saturated and highly negative media universe is both dangerous and foolish.

## A QUICK, YET IMPORTANT POINT OF CLARIFICATION

I know that several of my peers in the marketing and sales industry will scratch their heads initially as to the direction of this book compared to my first two. And I'm fine with that. It would have probably been safer, easier and less hassle to crank out another marketing and sales book, but my heart and soul are telling me that this is the right direction to expand and venture into. I'm confident that the "old pros" will pick up some fresh nuggets of wisdom in these pages, but my intention with the book is specifically to help the masses of people who've never been exposed to this type of powerful, life-changing knowledge.

Many of the strategies we'll explore are timeless. But I've also pulled from my own life experiences and from other achievers that I've studied, interviewed or have worked with directly to reveal several new strategies to improve your life and point you in the right direction. I have massive respect for my peers such as the timeless master Napoleon Hill and his modern day equivalent Jack Canfield, as they have influenced me greatly. However, this is not an attempt to recreate what they've written or rehash an epic novel of 1000+ pages containing every tip known to God and man.

The journey of discovery, learning and self improvement has been intensified greatly in my own life, in the last few years. I will continue until I take my final breath and are called from this place to meet the keeper of all knowledge - God. I will tell you upfront that writing this book has not been easy. Capturing and editing it down into its final form has been, at the same time, both challenging and a true labor of love. I'm highly aware that many excellent books have already been written on the topic of success throughout history and these pages are my best interpretation and perspective on a relevant topic at a unique and important time in our economic history.

A few months back, I was on the phone with a fellow marketing guru describing the outline of this book, and he summed up to me the direction and content of this, the third book in the Mind Capture book series, as being a "prequel." I nodded my head and agreed with his initial assessment.

**Prequel**: A work that supplements a previously completed one and has an earlier time setting.

I've noticed with clients, audiences and readers of my books, articles, and blogs a growing hunger for a change from status quo thinking. I have witnessed an incredible reaction when describing why the combination of a strong, well programmed success mindset and world class marketing skills are a perfect 1-2 punch in this quickly changing economy. Just as air and water are vital to human existence, these two combined skill sets are vital for sustained personal and business success.

### WILL THE <u>REAL</u> LEADERS PLEASE STEP UP AND BE RECOGNIZED?

In the past couple of years, I've seen fear creep into the minds of those whom I have least expected. Many supposed leaders from the for profit and non-profit worlds have titles indicating they're in charge, but they are telling a different story with their language, actions and mindset. In a time of challenge, many of them are playing the excuse game and showing little, if any, leadership ability. They continue to parade the cliché excuses as to why they're not leading or stepping up to solve problems. They talk a good game of double speak, under legal counsel's advice or through their board, often serving as a trained puppet. With these so-called leaders afraid to speak the truth and convey their real feelings, people are growing restless and starting to read through the BS.

I'm concerned. It appears on the surface that we've lost our groove, our bravado and faith in our talents, and the best economic model still around is known as capitalism. When tragedy, deranged killers, high speed car chases, foolish reality TV shows and negative opinions about free markets have taken precedence over achievement and good news stories with *most* media outlets, we're on a dangerous course.

## IF YOU STAND FOR NOTHING, YOU'LL FALL FOR ANYTHING

On the contrary, in this challenged marketplace and time of great economic change, I firmly believe that more and more people are awakening from the fog and beginning to question conventional programming ways of doing business and how they view their own skills and talents. I have faith and confidence that the ideas and strategies contained in this book, if implemented, can be the match to set on fire many new and worn down minds and awaken the world for greater good. It's time to fight back, re-gain control of our own lives and reshape our thoughts and attitudes. It's time to turn the tables and put mediocrity, complacency, apathy and fear on the defense. I'm excited to get this book and its message out to you and the rest of the world.

## Let's Address The Elephant In The Room Quickly:

We're in a recession; however, most people are sick of hearing about it. This book is designed to counter the excuses in your life and help you move beyond them into a solution-based, positive mindset to improve your own life and those you serve at home and in the marketplace.

The best visual I can give you to relate how most businesses, big and small, are treating the current economy, is to picture someone driving a moped at 30 MPH on the Autobahn freeway and wondering why people are blowing by them at light speed. They not only have the wrong vehicle, but they also are moving much too slowly in relation to their competition. The odds of catching up are slim to none unless they make adjustments in strategy and invest in a faster vehicle.

Many of the ideas and strategies contained in this book will not make the six o'clock news or be fully debated on all the talk radio and TV news programs. Here's the main reason why: **They aren't fear based**. My belief is that if you aren't completely sold on yourself, you'll risk losing the discipline and passion needed to hit your goals and achieve the life YOU DESIGN. This may sound strange at first, but you'll quickly discover why this is to your advantage to quickly accept and fully understand.

## WHAT'S THE PRIMARY GOAL OF THIS BOOK?

The answer is simple. In a direct and provocative way, help you reclaim your mind, confidence and entrepreneurial genius by sharing proven strategies to awaken your mental prowess in a world that's become addicted to fear, scarcity thinking, the status quo and the quick dismissal of people's talents. This isn't a special episode of Oprah or The View. It's far more important than that. I'm talking about the valuable and unique thing too many people take for granted: their own life.

> *"Those who program themselves for success find a way to succeed even in the most difficult of circumstances. Solutions to most problems come from one source and one source alone: yourself."*
> **-Napoleon Hill**

It's time to remove the shackles, take charge and reclaim your mind by playing an entirely different game that the top 5% of people play. This is frankly too small of a number and one I am committed to increase.

*"When the student is ready, the teacher will appear."*

The clues to a better mind and finding your inner genius to achieve your biggest goals have always been present. However, what I'm about to reveal is quite controversial as to why it's often harder and harder for most people to awaken and discover their true talents. Some of the reasons include:

- Guilt and conflicting philosophies about success which often confuse and distract the mind
- The massive amount of messaging and how to sort through the massive amounts of new information in the digital age which often creates confusion and burns up valuable time
- Powerful organizations and social structures in the political, religious and university arenas that still preach many outdated, fear-based and 'play-it-safe' ideas and belief structures
- An incredibly negative, invasive and fear-based, 24x7, media
- Unhappy people you may associate with who will do their best to lower your expectations and suppress your talents including family members, friends, peers and co-workers
- The glaring lack of focus on the importance of personal development and responsibility in our society
- As I've noted in the first two Mind Capture books, we're fully engaged in the age of constant distraction, shortened attention spans and real-time Internet connectivity which is, in many instances, doing more harm than good

Time and time again these mental shackles or inner conflicts outlined above take years to cleanse out of the mind and must be reprogrammed with new and improved mental software. How do I know this? I've lived it and continue to work at doing these things myself on a daily basis.  If it isn't done properly, many people find themselves on an emotional roller coaster of ups and downs and can't figure out why history keeps repeating itself.  Like a car stuck in neutral, their life energy and talents are greatly diminished.

## A KEY REMINDER BEFORE YOU ROLL UP
## YOUR SLEAVES AND DIG INTO THESE PAGES

Your mind is incredibly powerful whether you know it yet or not, and in the next few chapters, we'll dive into the mindset first. Within later chapters, we discuss several proven ways to demolish old, disempowering beliefs to help reprogram your mind for excellence. What a novel idea. **Excellence versus mediocrity and fear.** How enlightening and overdue! In a complex and rapidly changing world and economy, it's time to bring excellence and inner genius back to the forefront of people's lives, to not only cultivate their talents and ideas, but do it faster than imagined so the emerging economy and world might benefit sooner than later.

I am grateful and honored you have decided to invest your time, money and attention with the wisdom, stories, energy and exercises contained in this book to awaken and reshape your mind. It's my belief and conviction that you owe it to yourself to reclaim and improve upon your own genius to make the world a better place for not just you but those you wish to positively influence now and in the future. We may have not met before, but please make sure to check back with me online or at a live event on your successes and breakthroughs. One of the highest compliments a writer is blessed to receive is feedback from others who've invested their time and resources to positively change their own life and those around them for the better.

The economic battlefield is heating up and shows no signs of slowing down. We need to send positive, well-trained and awakened soldiers to the entrepreneurial front lines quickly. Consider this book as your own personal 'stimulus' plan that you create and which will serve as a guide for yourself, despite what the media, politicians and others think. Welcome to the boot camp for your mind!

# SECTION 1:

## MIND Clearing – Letting Go of Negative Mental Baggage

# CHAPTER 1:
# Permission To Go On The Offense

*"If you're attacking, you don't get as tired as when you're chasing."*

HAVE WE LOST OUR GROOVE? If you ask most people today, it appears we have. With the continual focus on how bad things are economically, I'm extremely troubled at the apathy and lack of leadership by many people—especially captains of industry and non-profit leaders and, in particular, the media.

Case in point: Good economic news has become minimized, downplayed and relegated to the sideline in most news circles within the media landscape. In addition, hard news is becoming more and more homogenized and incestuous where media pros are blending in more entertainment stories and 'breaking news' from the AP newswires and one or two other outlets. After many talks with publicists and business leaders, I can tell you with certainty that good economic news is often ignored or looked at with shock or disbelief.

Yes, there are challenges with the current economy. I call Michigan home and trust me, I've seen more economic carnage up close and personal the last few years within the auto and real estate sectors, in particular, than should humanly be allowed. It's easy and addictive for many people and the media to default on what we're doing wrong versus covering the smarter alternative of **what we're doing right**. However, in spite of the drum beat of intense economic fear being spewed forth amongst the media landscape, there are still people working, businesses carrying on and new businesses starting up each and every day. We humans are a resilient bunch indeed!

### An interesting observation regarding human nature

I've been noticing lately that many people are waiting around for someone to tell them to get busy and reassure them that everything will get better soon. Wake up people! You control your own destiny. As one of my heroes Jim Rohn so eloquently states, *no one can do your pushups for you*. Simple, yet powerful advice that's direct, timeless and easy to understand.

<u>Urgent and Breaking  MIND CAPTURE News Flash</u>
<u>That Will Probably Not Make The Newswires or Evening News</u>
<u>That You Should Read and Take Seriously:</u>

**Controversial entrepreneur and bestselling author chooses to buck the trend and not participate in the recession and advocates to ALL clients, readers and live audiences that neither should they!**

It's time for you to take the reins and go on the offense! No more waiting, speculating or hesitating. Your life and time are like a fuse, short and burning fast. You can't call timeout. The game's on. We need you to check back into the game and become the star. I don't say this to be morbid or negative, but frankly to kick you right in the butt to help you find your passion, or as my good friend John DiLemme calls it 'Your Why'. The stakes are high. The time is now. Not tomorrow. Not when your review is coming up. Not when you 'find more time'. Not when the time is right. Right now is the best time to get started.

**<u>I'll throw the gauntlet down right now and challenge you:</u>**
**IT'S TIME FOR <u>YOU</u> TO GO ON THE OFFENSE!**

I've been challenging live audiences the last several months by telling them directly and without reservation that NOW is the time to go on the offense! They need to grab the reins, step up and quit making excuses or buying into the excuses that seem to be everywhere they turn. I give them permission to go on the offense and to look at the world much differently and with a fresh mind in such areas as:

- Growing their business
- Trying new sales and marketing techniques
- Ignoring the media hype and pundits
- Setting a new direction for their life
- Moving ahead with their goals, dreams and plans without waiting for others' approval
- Becoming a merchant of hope to others and, in particular, their customers and employees
- Having their best year ever by solving more problems within the marketplace
- Associating with achievers by hanging out with eagles and not pigeons
- Improving their life, career and business when most people say you can't or it's impossible

As the first nine months of 2010 have marched into the pages of history, I've found myself becoming more and more challenged — no that's too kind, I'll say *deeply disturbed* — when watching the news, listening to most people and reading magazines and newspapers online and offline for leisure and research purposes. It seems that most of the time, the media's advocating that people should retreat, play it safe, give up, feel bad about others stupidity and sadly settle for less with their lives.

Being in the marketing and sales industry for most of my life, I think to ignore the messaging and power of the media's influence is a dangerous thing to do. Far too many self-help gurus preach this, and I disagree with them most of the time. If you plan to engage the media with your story, mission and message, it's a smart idea to know what makes them tick. I believe without a doubt that many folks have lost faith and confidence in not only the economy but, more importantly, in themselves and that it CAN be reversed, diminished and replaced with a new and improved mindset.

### Pundit Mentality to Be Aware of and Learn From

Most online, TV and talk radio pundits, regardless of political slant or bias, are masters at cranking up emotions and hot air with their audiences. Since they have a forum to spout their views, I'll weigh in right now with my own two cents.

**THE PROBLEM:** They get you fired up, ready to march with pitchforks in the street, but then they rarely offer up positive and constructive solutions. I call this 'Big talk and little action' media in full force. In Texas they say, *big hat – no cattle.*

**THE SOLUTION:** Believe in yourself and get busy changing your own situation for the better before joining the ranks of pundits and unhappy masses which are eager to complain, yet do little of anything to change, take positive action or offer up constructive solutions.

Relentless negative news, massive denial and the wrong mindset are clearly taking their toll, and the casualties of economic war are mounting faster each day in the form of job losses, lost profits and established businesses of all shapes and sizes going under. It's time for people to stop adding fuel to the fire and step up to not only improve their own life, but those they seek to serve and positively influence. The goal is to inspire, motivate and fire people up with a unique message of trusting in their talents and dreams with proven ways to stay up in a down world.

### A Common Thread in High Achievers That May Shock You

I've been blessed to meet, train, learn from and associate with many high-achievers from around the globe. One thing that they all agree on is the power of association. And more importantly, many aso believe in feeding their mind with positive information. "Shockingly" as the media would say, many of them have never attended college or even finished high school, but their capacity for continual, life-long learning is unmatched.

On the other hand, I've also met and spoken to many MBAs and academic types that reek of arrogance, elitism and 'know-it-all' thinking. And frankly, it's toxic to even be in the same room with them. They're often book smart without question; however, life and commerce are not conducted just in the college classroom. The customer of today doesn't issue us a grade or let us turn them into a case study. They either choose to do business with us or they don't. Second place translates into lost business and opportunity.

Let's go back in time for just a moment to the early 1990s when I was studying business in college. I ran into an old friend on summer break and the encounter forever changed my destiny. He explained that he was part of a 'business opportunity' that I should take a look at. As you might be guessing, it was a network marketing company. I ended up joining and doing fairly well for a 20-year old college student. I was in the company for only a year, but the experience changed one major thing for the rest of my life: How I looked at and viewed the world. Positive books, people and personal development were introduced into my life. Thank God.

Why wasn't I learning or even aware of this 'other world of thinking' in high school or college? Regardless of whether you love or despise the network marketing industry, they are masters at changing the mindset of the typical, or in my case – uninformed – person into someone different. No, not the one who chases you down at a family reunion to show you how to make millions and quit your job. I'm talking about someone who becomes exposed to successful people and, most importantly, the mindset and goal-setting strategies needed to achieve greater success in multiple facets of their life.

### The Right Mindset Is Critical to Success

So why does the direct sales industry relentlessly focus on reprogramming the mind for achievement? There's no one size fits all answer but here's my best rationale: They know that the initial excitement and momentum will quickly wane and drop off, unless training and immersion into positive training, books and support structures (upline) are quickly put into place if the new recruit is to have any shot at not only sticking with the business but achieving long-term success. Let's look at six typical challenges that the typical person in this industry faces when they get started:

1. Lots of rejection
2. Confusion and criticism from those who are often closest to them
3. Negative perceptions that are often untrue about the industry or company they've joined
4. **A big shift in mindset to becoming pro-active and entrepreneurial**
5. Creation of new habits and better time management skills to achieve advancement
6. The old 'get-rich-quick' mentality most people still have in their minds

Not many people will look at this list and get excited. Similar to the focus of this book, I've highlighted the fourth challenge on the list because this industry is well aware of the power of the positive mind. Here are five essential books that ALL students of personal development should read and apply within their lives:

- *The Bible*
- *Think & Grow Rich*
- *The Richest Man in Babylon*
- *The Success Principles*
- *The Greatest Salesman In the World*

I'm amazed at how many people have heard of these books and still refuse to either get them or even read them. I have a business rule that you might find instructive. When millions of high achievers continually recommend books that have changed their lives for the better, it's a smart idea to investigate and check out for myself why these high achievers speak so highly about them.

In the next chapter, we'll look at why so many people and businesses are quickly exiting the competitive landscape and what you can do to avoid this. You'll be shocked at some of the reasons why it's happening and why most people never see it coming until it's too late.

## CHAPTER 2:
# Casualties of Economic War

*"If we do not hang together,*
*we will most assuredly, hang separately."*
- Benjamin Franklin

As I STEPPED UP AND REACHED over to insert my key into the outside door to my office, I glanced to my left and froze for a few seconds. I noticed that the real estate office 20 yards away was now an empty building. I then looked around at all the other spaces that had recently joined the list of deceased former businesses in my town: the restaurant directly across the street that had been closed for many months and the local builder next door who had been the newest addition to our community had placed the 'Closed' sign in the window for the last time under the cover of night to avoid the shame of exiting the business community under dire conditions.

These three former businesses had high hopes and big expectations when they started, but now all that's left are empty buildings, overgrown landscaping and carefully placed "For Sale" signs scattered around the property to serve as visual reminders that the casualties of economic war are surrounding my business.

I've often thought that when I'm having an off day or feeling a little less motivated than normal, all I have to do is look out the window of my office for a quick dose of visual motivation to keep the business battle waging. Yes, a strange mental picture to open up chapter two, but an important one to remind us that every business can and will face challenges.

### Why Did These Former Businesses Become Casualties of Economic War?

I have my suspicions as to what took these three businesses out of the game. A variety of things added up to the demise of these businesses with the final deathblow being a major slowdown in overall business for these three industries as a whole which they weren't prepared to handle. In my opinion, this is only a minor symptom to the greater illness. Here's my assessment. All three shared great locations, so traffic and letting people know where to find them and letting people know what they offered weren't issues. To this day, they still have other competitors who are still in business and plugging away. At the end of the day, it is my belief that they closed due to three central reasons:

1.  Lack of new customers
2.  Lack of repeat business
3.  **Lack of belief in themselves**

The first two challenges are faced by every business on the planet. This is a given. In the first two *Mind Capture* books, we cover multiple ways to handle these two challenges. The third challenge is the 'dirty secret' that most people deny or downplay within their business which is the mental battle in their own mind. Again, the book you now hold in your hands is arguably the missing link needed to help you truly get ahead and stay ahead for the long haul. If you don't believe in yourself and let fear and doubt creep into your mind, eventually it will take over and dominate your thoughts.

The first two challenges in business described above increase with greater speed and intensify during a recession. As competition for sales and repeat business increases, here are two common mistakes business and non-profit organizations make that you must avoid:

1.  **CUTTING BACK ON MARKETING**
2.  **LITTLE OR NO PERSONAL DEVELOPMENT OR ONGOING TRAINING**

Hiding in a bunker is a common practice advocated by many bean counters, tenured professors and overly cautious business owners who want to wait out a recession. I believe this is a recipe for disaster. The best visual comparison I can give is slow, self-induced suffocation. The decision was made to take on 'penny wise, pound foolish' thinking by many people internally and outside consultants who have never had to meet a payroll. They are usually not qualified to dispense marketing advice. This is like me asking a top heart doctor to create a three-step direct mail campaign for one of my clients and me stepping into the ER to perform heart valve replacement surgery with zero training. The results would be catastrophic for everyone involved.

I also strongly caution and urge you to resist the temptation to cut back on not only marketing but **investing** in training for yourself and your staff. Top companies, regardless of industry, are big believers in ongoing training. Sadly, too many small and mid-size businesses see it only as an expense on their balance sheet without really looking at all the dividends it pays.

If marketing and having the proper mindset are the oxygen of every healthy organization, why do people continue to cut off the air supply? They then wonder why a potent combination of poor repeat sales, sinking employee morale, a lack of new sales and less than stellar results with their marketing efforts are the result. What did they expect?

*"Invest in your mind, for it's the one thing no one*
*can take away from you."*
-Benjamin Franklin

I'm often accused by peers in my industry of being 'simplistic' with some of the techniques I share with audiences and in my writings. It doesn't bother me one bit as I know they work. What I'm most concerned with are sustained results. When fleshing out the outline and focus of this book, the common issue that kept popping up as a major challenge to ongoing business success was the lack of attention given by many of my peers to the importance of not only having a positive mindset, but effective ways to sharpen and maintain it during this time of great economic change.

### So What's The Biggest Enemy To Most Businesses Right Now? The Answer Might Surprise You.

A huge new threat has snuck in the back door of most businesses, and most sales and marketing gurus are underestimating it. Its name? Fear. I'm seeing lots of people working harder than ever to maintain or even grow sales but often running into an invisible brick wall caused by mental self sabotage and then wondering why they often feel 'stuck'. The problem can almost always be traced back to the wrong mindset and lack of mental training to increase the odds of them staying focused, motivated and ready to conquer the challenges in achieving success.

Yes, superior marketing tactics are very important. I'm not abandoning my marketing roots with this book. However, based on the changing battlefield conditions of commerce, most people and businesses will have a very tough road ahead if their mindset isn't equally as prepared for the new threat known as fear changing the rules of engagement. Some companies will send their people to the occasional seminar or training, but here's the painful reality: **It will often <u>not</u> produce sustained, positive, long-term change**. It's better than nothing, but for long-term change to occur, it has to be consistent and the desired outcomes and changes should be tracked and monitored.

It's a mirage. An illusion designed to make people think they've learned all they need to know until next year. Similar to a struggling person on a yo-yo diet where their weight swings up and down, the mental ebbs and flows are critical to work on improving each day. The media and your competition aren't getting any nicer. This is a fact.

I make no apologies for going a bit negative here. But if your career, customers and business are important to you, then it's time to step up and push yourself to a new level of understanding and mental growth. No sugar coating or coddling allowed. You're an adult, so let's keep rolling. As we move into chapter three and subsequent chapters, the primary objective is to share with you several effective ways to not only keep yourself up mentally in an increasingly negative world, but to also explain how to implement and make them into powerful new habits. We'll also look at the traits that high achievers share that you can learn from to jump ahead and improve your life for the better.

## Why We Need You to Step Up More Than Ever

As I mastermind with fellow business associates and other agents of positive change from around the globe, we all agree on one major thing: The world has a long list of challenges that will need a new mindset and different approaches to solve. We'll need more people to roll up their sleeves and get into the game. The challenge is great and the time is now. The only way this is possible is through inspired people driven by passion and who are ready to hustle, take charge, leave excuses behind and create new solutions in spite of the loud chorus of critics and negative, fear-based media throwing road blocks in the way. We need to enlist you to help us wage the battle.

## Bail Yourself Out and Stop Looking for a Handout

At the end of the day when you look in the mirror at yourself, you must understand that long-term happiness and success, depending on how you define them, cannot be simply bought or given to you as a handout. It starts with you and grows outward. Confident, goal-driven, focused and consistent achievers already understand this. The goal again of this book is to engage, disrupt, challenge and shake up old and ineffective beliefs and thoughts and replace them with positive habits and strategies to make positive change a daily part of your life.

## A Simple Equation That You Must Awaken In Your Mind
### Forced Redistribution of Wealth = Theft

It's in fashion these days for people to want something for nothing and it's not only killing the economy, but it's also taking away healthy and perfectly capable people's ability to think, innovate and empower themselves to seek ways to provide for themselves versus passing the buck onto someone else. It's of little help that our current political environment encourages endless entitlement programs that shuffle money from one person's pocket to another.

If you or I attempted to do what both parties of Congress are currently doing with many of their laws and proposed policies in the private sector to our fellow neighbors or business associates, we'd quickly be locked up on trumped up charges, vilified and instantly discredited by the media machine. Regardless of Congress's games, at the end of the day, creating wealth and pursuing your passion and dreams is up to you, and only you. I'll spare you a course on economics, supply and demand bell curves, and instead lay out two more simple and direct equations as they relate to entitlement thinking:

**Focused Excuses and Blame = Status Quo and Bitterness**
**Focused Action and Responsibility = Positive Results and Freedom**

Which equation best describes you? The aim of this book is to get and keep you operating in the second equation to not only live a better life, but also turn the tide against the sea of folks who are wasting their talents and also negatively influencing others at the same time. It's interesting how much precious time and mental space is occupied by focusing on excessive fear and doubt, over analyzing the past, and blaming others within most people's minds. Your own self-talk conversations are either moving you forward, keeping you stuck or holding you back in time. Here's a wonderful quote from author Gay Hendricks to expand your mental paradigm:

*"When you reach the end of your life and are wondering whether it's all been worthwhile, you'll be measuring whether you did everything you possibly could with all the gifts you've been given."*

It's mind boggling to meet and see unhappy people who complain and carry on about how bad things are, but they can tell you with a smile on their face in vivid detail all the gossip about co-workers, family, friends and of course all the reality TV shows they watch hours on end each day. It's bizarre that they take their own life force, energy, talents, and valuable time and waste it in front of the TV or computer. It's almost like their life is a twisted episode of the classic TV show, *The Twilight Zone*, where reality and fantasy are warped together with the victim unaware that the joke is on them. The numbers don't lie. The average North American watches more than four hours of TV or online driven media per day. No wonder why we have so many "average" and unhappy people these days within our society.

### A Warning About Hope

Hope is an interesting word. I believe that too much hope in people's lives is dangerous. For example, staying upbeat and having hope while you're taking action is fine by me. When you remove the action and rely only on hope, you're setting yourself up for a life of frustration. Far too many people are hoping that things get better in their life, but they're unwilling to learn new skills, change their habits, listen to new ideas or take a different course of action to increase the odds that things will change for the better.

Discipline and hard work aren't sexy or easy to peddle in an age of instant gratification. A lot of motivational speakers miss this one or minimize that designing and achieving the life you desire is not going to be easy at first. You can't rely on "attracting" your way to success only. Yes, I'm a proud Mid-Westerner and we call this new age, 'woo-woo' thinking. Sounds nice, but where's the beef? Remember: Nothing happens unless you take action! This is and WILL always remain the first and most important step in the process.

I often challenge people in my live seminars and keynote addresses with the statement that hope is not a marketing strategy. They laugh, but I'm not kidding. Most small and mid-sized businesses and sales professionals have no real game plan as it relates to their marketing. They coast when times are good and panic when things tighten up. The same thing I see in marketing is even harder to find when it comes to people taking charge of their lives and mapping out an action plan to better living.

Here's a helpful list I've created to aid and keep you on track when it comes to marketing. I recommend you photocopy this page and post these commandments where you can see and reference back to on a regular basis.

## The 10 'MIND CAPTURE' Marketing COMMANDMENTS

*Thou shall give thanks each day to your customers who provide income and employment*

*Thou shall know that marketing is the oxygen of every growing organization*

*Thou shall customize your messages to connect and engage prospects and customers*

*Thou shall understand that complacency in marketing = slow death*

*Thou shall seek out wise books, seminars, associations and mastermind partners to learn new wisdom and ideas to stay ahead*

*Thou shall understand that 'hope' is not a marketing strategy*

*Thou shall communicate with and educate key customers, prospects and referral partners on a consistent basis*

*Thou shall employ and use fun and humor to avoid the #1 sin in marketing: being boring*

*Thou shall not whine and complain about the economy, but seek to find solutions and add more value to your current product or service*

*Thou shall track all sacred leads by asking "How did you hear about us?"*

Now, let's move into chapter three where the battle we all wage within our minds, called self-talk, is in full swing by looking under the microscope at how it positively or negatively influences and shapes our view of the world. We'll see if you're tough enough to press on in achieving your goals or if you'll resign your fate to giving up at the first sign of resistance. This is where the true boot camp to build a stronger mind begins.

## CHAPTER 3:
# If They Only Knew

*"What would you do if you knew*
*you could not fail?"*

THIS IS A SIMPLE, YET POWERFUL quote from the past that's relevant to start our next lesson. I often find when I listen to, see or meet a person who's struggling or has given up on his or her goals and dreams a phrase that pops into my mind that I'll share with you now. I find my inner voice saying, *if they only knew*. So what do I mean by this statement? I'll explain.

I believe that if people could fight through the mental clutter of doubt, disbelief, fear, past challenges and negative opinions from others they would be amazed at the power and inner genius they possess. Their talents and creative genius have been buried and need to be reclaimed and put into action. Here are a few common obstacles holding back people and how I'd reframe the challenge if they asked for my advice:

19

- *If they only knew that starting a business is possible and could positively change their destiny*
- *If they only knew that when a door closes a new one opens if they're prepared to go through it*
- *If they only knew that by getting good at marketing, sales and communication it could allow them to serve far more people than they ever imagined*
- *If they only knew how blessed they already are they would be grateful for what they have instead of focusing on what they don't have*
- *If they only knew that most of their fears will never happen or materialize*
- *If they only knew how valuable time is they'd push themselves harder and with greater urgency*

**Bottom Line:** *If they only knew what they could accomplish by believing in themselves!*

I look at each person as a unique, one-of-a-kind marvel created by God with massive potential and talents. When we're children, we envision lives of possibility and wonder why adults are so boring and always telling us "no" and that we should "be realistic." I have three kids and they are masters of possibility and creativity. The world is a wide open mystery full of excitement and questions. In my second book, I explain why they are hands down the best sales people in the world. For starters, they're relentless, determined, creative and persistent. Unfortunately, most adults have forgotten why these are important traits to keep and use each day.

But what happens to most children when they grow up? By their late teens and early twenties, three central enemies begin to creep in and slowly take over most people's lives and minds. They appear harmless at first, however. I'm going to explain why they are often the biggest challenges grown adults face when designing a life of significance and positive change. They are:

1. Habit force
2. Views on security and risk
3. Fear of rejection

Before we cover the danger these three enemies often present, I need to rewind the clock for just a minute to help prove my premise.

## <u>Anything</u> is Possible!
## A Short Trip Back in Time to Prove it.

Here's the good news: you are allowed to change. I've seen change in many eagles with whom I have had the honor to be associated, and I've lived change up close and personal the last 15 years. I've included in the back of this book a special FREE bonus to receive two audio interviews with Dr. Ivan Misner and Jack Canfield whom I interviewed for my monthly newsletter, *A Captured Mind*. This offer not only adds more value to your investment in this book, but I also want to share with you their insights about success.

Between the ages of 20 to 37, I had three entirely different career changes. I started on the proverbial factory floor in my twenties punching out parts on second and third shifts for the automotive industry, then progressed to door-to-door sales in two of the most competitive and arguably disliked industries, telecom and advertising, to penning a bestselling book and starting two businesses in my early thirties and advising leaders in the boardroom. What an amazing trip for the youngest of nine kids in a blended, middle-class family in which both sides of my family worked for GM during its heyday. I share this timeline not to boast, but to inspire you and paint a richer perspective that anything is possible if you're driven, motivated and work tirelessly on improving yourself each and every day.

Hard work and applying yourself does and still can pay off. The founders of this country waged a life and death battle to prove it. Sadly, many people would have you believe that this great country offers little or diminished opportunities. There are countless stories of first generation immigrants who still come here with lots of disadvantages and end up becoming multimillionaires and valuable role models within their communities.

### What Happened To The Good Old Fashioned Hero?

I designed this book to serve as both a road map and resource guide to teach you how this massive change in career, income and evolution took place and to show you the mentors, skills, knowledge and mindset required to achieve success. I'm done being politically correct. Far too many motivational speakers and authors in my profession are afraid to truly speak their mind on how to overcome adversity for fear of possibly offending someone. I believe that it's time for you to speak your mind without constant fear of someone being offended. I'd rather speak my passion and ideas than cower in fear and regret.

It is my belief and observation from meeting thousands of people in my travels that the market is begging for and seeking out authenticity, answers and good resources to better their situation in an age of cynicism and continual negative news stories loading up the cable talk show dial and blogosphere. Lately, a lot of people ranging from star athletes and politicians to supposed business leaders and everyday people are doing extremely stupid things or staged media stunts in hopes of possible fame on YouTube or to land a reality show appearance with a six-figure book deal waiting in the wings.

I don't like or buy most people's excuses. As a father of three children, I can tell you that kids are good at this because they either don't know better or they're testing your limits to see what they can get away with. How tragic it is today that we have a large number of adults, who like most teenagers, are experts at making excuses as to why they didn't get their homework assignment or chores done and treat their adult lives the same way. Psychologists and 'wanna be' experts analyze and parade out reasons why it's acceptable to be upset and that it's not really their fault. This is pure BS and excuse making. Let's call it what it is.

To add fuel to the fire, many unhappy people find that misery loves company via a willing accomplice known as the media that welcomes them on TV, radio, print and online forums to discuss their challenges (aka: excuses) over and over, and over again to a large segment of society that sadly nods its collective head in agreement looking for sympathy. This low level and toxic pattern of thinking needs to begin changing quickly or the casualties of economic war will continue to mount.

Let's take a closer look at the three central challenges grown adults face when designing a life of significance and positive change.

**Challenge #1: Habit force.** The old adage that we are 'creatures of habit' is right on. While some habits are good, many adults have habits that are holding them back which must be replaced if they intend to create a positive life of significance. Here are several habits related to mindset to avoid and new habits to replace them with. With patience and common sense often in short supply these days, I urge you to grab a pen right now and review both lists carefully and circle the top two areas you believe that need to be improved upon in your own life.

| Runner Up mindset habits: | Champion mindset habits: |
| --- | --- |
| Making excuses | Get things done on time |
| Easily distracted | Focused |
| Inconsistent | Able to hit deadlines |
| Disorganized and waste time | In control and efficient |
| Blame others | Personal responsibility |
| Stop learning | Learn new things each day |
| Engage in gossip | Look for the good in each situation |
| Too much TV and Internet | Limited amount of TV and Internet time |
| Associate with negative people | Hang around positive people |
| Laziness | Fierce, passionate and determined |
| Shy | Confident and assertive |

**Assignment:** Circle the top two areas you need to improve upon. Now, in the area below, write down the new steps you'll take starting today to change these mindset habits for the better.

_____

_____

_____

_____

_____

Why did I have you write down the changes you're going to make? The answer is simple. It's proven that when you write something down the odds significantly increase in your favor that you'll take action. While it takes 21 days to create a new habit, you have to take the first step right now and write down what you seek to change. I encourage you to think on paper regularly. For my younger readers, I urge you to disconnect from the iPod, cell phone and computer and grab a pen and paper. It's a timeless skill that high achievers use in many facets of their lives to not only solve problems, but map out and capture new ideas and opportunities as well.

**Challenge #2: Views on security and risk.** Why do people still subscribe to this outdated and limiting concept of "security"? The three major groups still pushing this outdated concept and thinking process are politicians, the media and academia. A quick disclaimer: I have no axe to grind with any particular person in any of these three groups. I know a fair number of good politicians, reporters and university professionals. Wait! There is one person I'll name from my home state who really challenges me. Michael Moore would be the exception to this rule. Enough said. However, politicians, the media and higher education as a whole still push and sell people on the notions of safety and security within three major areas of life including:

1. Jobs and Careers
2. Money and finances
3. Creativity

### Security Is a Lie

What I'm about to share next may upset you so brace yourself. As I have evolved from the factory floor to the boardroom, my initial beliefs about security and taking risks related to employment have been turned upside down. I've learned many things at each stage of my career that I wouldn't trade as they've shaped and taught me many powerful lessons. In addition, they've given me a wonderful gift called perspective.

The thinking and opinions advocated while in college from many tenured academics telling me to get a 'good job with good benefits' to my fellow coworkers on the factory floor telling me to play it safe while at the same time demanding higher pay and better benefits simply won't work anymore. They have no merit or validity in the new economy of innovation and direct global competition. They're an illusion still being peddled by far too many entitlement-driven politicians, working with a cadre of willing accomplices in many media newsrooms and academic institutions. They choose to ignore reality and are in complete denial of the new economy and massive changes in thinking and economics taking place right in front of their eyes.

Old school 20th century elitism, ivory tower thinking and 'something for nothing' viewpoints are sadly still being pushed, packaged and advocated to the 'working class'. This is about as silly as a grown adult still believing that the Easter Bunny exists! Here's the problem with this antiquated mindset: people are starting to wake up, question and challenge the old guard and status quo. In addition, the Internet and its revolutionary changes to communication are crumbling the pillars of old institutions second-by-second, one blog post, one tweet, one email and one YouTube video at a time.

*"The truth is incontrovertible. Malice may attack it.*
*Ignorance may deride it. But, in the end there it is."*
-Sir Winston Churchill

Is it any wonder why so many politicians, reporters and academic leaders look so frustrated, confused and worried these days? You can read many of their faces and body language and see that they're often lying through their teeth or holding back what they'd really like to say. The revolution in thinking has started and a new game is being played. The old views on safety and security are being torn down and rebuilt in ways that they can't believe, fathom or control for much longer.

**Challenge #3: The fear of rejection.** By the time the average person hits 18 years of age, he or she has heard the word "no" at a bare minimum of 12,000 – 15,000 times based on various sources. It's amazing how many people quit before they even get started with trying to pursue a major goal. They usually let a potent combination of other people's opinions, excuses and negative mental self-talk sabotage their drive, ideas and talents.

Why do so many adults give up so easily? Have we become that sensitive and scared when it comes to dealing with adversity and challenges? I often ask these questions to myself and shake my head in disbelief when I hear, see or meet someone who's given up on life and pursuing his or her passion. We all know or have met someone who has a wonderful idea, talent or dream that's never been acted on or even pursued.

Here's a great example to prove that people give up too easily. I can't tell you how many people I meet who'd love to write a book. There are hundreds of thousands of books released each year. There are easily two to three times as many books that are still stuck in people's heads or in the dresser of a night stand that will never get written, finished, yet alone printed. When you ask these people how they're progressing, a variety of excuses flow from their mouth as to why they haven't gotten started or have decided to wait until next month, or next year. It's a shame and at the same time frustrating to witness.

I'm often told by others that I can be bold, direct, persistent, cocky and even obnoxious. I often answer this by saying "thank you" and consider their feedback or perception of me as a high compliment. You will discover that when you're chasing big goals and dreams that it will often scare and confuse many people. Fortune favors the bold and it's time people start stepping up and asking for more from themselves.

A couple of years ago, I had one of my central mentors send me a letter taking me to task for what he believed to be aggressive follow up with some of his business associates. We gladly worked things out and I learned a couple of things from the experience. I was initially shocked and frankly felt like I'd been sucker punched by his memo. However, thinking back on the situation today a couple years later, I'm actually not ashamed or embarrassed by my behavior. This type of tenacity and occasional "shoot first, apologize later" mentality is essential as an entrepreneur and also in life when pursuing your goals.

Once you master your mind and the power of focus, it will astound and even shock you as you'll begin to attract and draw in better opportunities for your life. In addition, you'll also telegraph to critics, doubters, 'dream-stealers' and competitors to either wake up and assist you or get out of the way. Yes, a few trees will get burned in the forest in your quest to awaken your entrepreneurial genius.

The moral of the story as it relates to pursuing your goals can be summed up best below:

**Life is short. The road to success is paved with lots of "NOs." You never, ever, ever know what can happen until you ask. I urge and challenge you to start asking for more. Quit waiting around and go on the offense!**

Now, let's turn the spotlight on deconstructing fear and discovering why its influence is so powerful and what you can do to address it, keep it in check and blast through it when it rears its ugly head. This next chapter will test and challenge many of your core beliefs and societal programming and norms. Prepare yourself and bring an open mind. There is light at the end of the tunnel.

# CHAPTER 4:
# The Culture of Fear

*You gain strength, courage, and confidence by each*
*experience in which you really stop to look fear in the face.*
*You are able to say to yourself, "**I have lived through***
***this horror. I can take the next thing that comes along.***"
Eleanor Roosevelt

WHAT DETERMINES, SHAPES AND influences your own fear factor? There are several things, but here are a few vital clues:

- What you watch, read and say to others
- What you've learned and believe
- What you think about the most
- What questions you ask
- What you do and the actions you take
- With whom you associate

So what do I mean by 'fear factor'? I'm not referring to the once popular TV show where physical skill and ability to gross out the audience by eating insects was packaged and sold as skill and entertainment, but something much more important. First, here's what I mean by fear factor: How you approach, handle and respond to risk whether real or imagined.

Everyone experiences fear. The challenge when fear presents itself is the game your mind begins to play. Your self-talk will begin to either support you or bring you down. Most people, when presented with an opportunity or fresh idea, will begin to shoot it down and come up with a list of reasons it can't be done, may not work or is simply "too risky." With the rapid changes in the economy and work, many of the old rules of engagement and thinking need to be thrown out the door.

The glaring problem most people have in the pursuit of their inner genius, and I base this on how few people within society are living fully engaged and on purpose, is that their inside and outside mental programming causes them to focus and default back to worst case scenarios over and over. Sadly, they often have no idea they're even doing it.

> *"Either you decide to stay in the shallow end of the pool,*
> *or you go out in the ocean."*
> -Christopher Reeve

Deflecting opportunities is a horrible habit to possess. Buried below the layers of negative behavior and programming, opportunity is sadly a foreign word in most people's vocabulary. I believe that fear is the silent, yet #1, enemy to most people on their journey to a life of significance. It's a convenient and comfortable trick of the mind which sets up the next dangerous habit known as excuse making. Fear and excuse making are closely linked together.

### The Three Primary Fear Peddlers You Must Be On Guard to Defend From Stealing Your Mind and Your Inner Genius

1. The media
2. Your associations
3. The marketplace

Let's take a closer look at these three areas where many fear peddlers congregate and identify key distinctions to help bullet-proof your mind and flush out toxic programming.

**#1. The media.** This should be an obvious one, yet far too many people diminish the media's influence on the mindset and ability to shape public opinion. The old adage in media rooms of "if it bleeds it leads" has taken over and dominates most news outlets. It's simply amazing to watch how news has been twisted into not only gossip and entertainment but also a forum to complain, plant fear (swine flu anyone?) and focus much more time than should be allowed on what's wrong with society, real or imagined, and rarely on what we're doing well.

I think the media's attitude can best be summed up in lyrics from the song *Villains* by the rock group Verve Pipe:

*I turned the volume up this morning*
*'Til there was ringing in my ears*
*I haven't felt this good in years*

*Another villain on the cover*
*Of every major magazine*
*The victim somewhere in between*

*See how they twist and shout*

As I criss-cross through airports, I occasionally catch fellow travelers (aka: zombies) glued upward watching the TV for the daily debate, "situation," protest or latest idiotic high-speed chase being covered from a chopper in the air high above a major city. **Most** of these folks do not look excited or happy as they view the visual parade of fear and human stupidity taking over their time and mind. It's not uncommon to see many shaking their head or mumbling under their breath with disgust.

When I'm teaching groups or meeting with retainer clients, I advise them that ignoring the media and its influence is foolish. Who do you want educating your customers and prospects? You or them (the media)? This is an easy answer, but many firms do little if any "counter-programming" to ensure that they have a voice and educate their customers. There are always two sides to every story, and you must aggressively make positive publicity a part of your marketing and promotional efforts.

If you're looking to influence and have any shot at reaching the media with good news or an alternative viewpoint to the headlines, it's smart to tap into the media's playbook and thinking. However, most people fit into one of two camps when it comes to media consumption. The first group spends far too much time online and offline hooked on breaking news, checking the weather, and getting pulled into minutia and "latest developments." The other group ignores the media and current trends, and this is just as dangerous. Balance is required. Be aware, but not addicted to the news.

Let's examine one form of media that's in the spotlight a lot these days: talk radio. This is a medium that's highly addictive and frankly, entertaining. Although I tune into it, I do caution you to not let it consume you. Many on-air hosts are masters of provocation and not so good at offering solutions. The primary goals here with this book are to make you aware of how to design your ideal life and also things to watch out for that can trip up or derail you in the quest to achieve it. You should make it your goal to focus most of your time and talents on things you can directly impact and control. Why waste valuable time and focus on "big issues" that often distract your mental progress and pursuit of the things you can directly influence? Again, be aware but don't let it consume you or bring you down.

**#2. Your associations.** Who you spend time with **does** have an impact on your life, thoughts and productivity. Many self-help gurus have said that they can guess your income within a few hundred dollars based on the top five people with whom you associate. Harsh? Unfair? Maybe. Frankly, I have to agree that this assessment is indeed accurate. Who you spend time with is extremely important in your quest to achieve a better life.

Monitor closely the time you spend with your family, friends, co-workers and business associates, as these are your most influential associations. I recommend you audit these three areas and list below the top five people you associate with and rank their attitude on a simple one to ten scale. One being negative, five being average and ten as positive and supportive most if not all the time. At the end of each year, I do a business inventory and reflect back on those who've had the biggest impact on my life. I highly suggest you do the same.

| **Family - Rank**<br>(Top 5 Assoc.) | **Friends - Rank**<br>(Scale of 1-10) | **Co-workers/Bus. Associates - Rank**<br>(Scale of 1-10) |
|---|---|---|
| 1._____ __ | 1._____ __ | 1._____ __ |
| 2._____ __ | 2._____ __ | 2._____ __ |
| 3._____ __ | 3._____ __ | 3._____ __ |
| 4._____ __ | 4._____ __ | 4._____ __ |
| 5._____ __ | 5._____ __ | 5._____ __ |

As I've gotten into my mid-thirties and evolved from the factory floor to the boardroom, I've noticed that many people from my twenties that I associated with are no longer in my top five lists. As a matter of fact, there are many people I haven't heard from in years. Some drift away with the passage of time, which is natural, while there are others I've deliberately chosen not to spend time with.

There's the classic saying that you can choose your friends but you can't choose your family. I'm going to urge you to think about that last statement very carefully. I do believe that if you have negative relatives in your life that you must remove them from your sphere of influence. Sounds harsh, but it's essential to set them and yourself free if they continue to bring you down.

Common clues that it's time to distance yourself include jealousy, continual negative comments and rehashing past incidents as if they're still relevant or real. You can still love them, but you have the power of choice to not hang around them.

## SLOW DOWN, TAKE A FEW MINUTES AND LOOK INWARD

Humans have the unique, God-given talent to self-reflect. It's stunning how little time and attention is given to this powerful gift. People often place higher priority on mapping out their annual vacation (short-term perspective) than they do mapping out and monitoring their life plan (long-term perspective) via self reflection and other strategies we'll discuss in later chapters. It also doesn't help that an entire new age of interruption and real-time access is making it harder and harder for people to slow down and focus.

Multitasking is popular and celebrated in most social circles. It's like a badge of honor to many people to harp on just how "busy" they are. I often think when I hear or read this, *busy doing what?* We've allowed a lot of the new technology to run us ragged and waste lots of productive time. Most high achievers I associate with are also masters of getting things done, without distraction, when necessary, and they defend their time like a hawk. You also might be shocked that many of them rarely check email or answer their mobile phone. The ability to meet deadlines is a powerful skill to get good at and stay good at. By limiting and controlling the intake of interruption, they get much more accomplished.

**#3. The marketplace.** Be on guard and aware of fear peddling in the opinions and comments from your competitors, non-profits and politicians. This should raise a few eye brows and that's good. As it relates to the economy and competition, lately it seems that most unsuccessful businesses would prefer to wallow in "me-too" thinking and the popular excuse of how bad the economy is. They can sound off with precision a litany of reasons their sales are slow and most of it is sadly based on excuses fueled by associations. Hopefully by now you see how these areas of influence, when unchecked, make it challenging for most people to achieve their goals.

Instead of being proactive, most people are in a negative and often reactionary state and don't even know why. If they spent as much time on solution-based thinking and taking action versus fear-based thinking, they would likely find themselves in a better situation, but more importantly in a better state of mind.

The second area in the marketplace to be keenly aware of is the influence of non-profits. Let me be clear here: I work with many non-profits that do a great job, deliver value to those in need and earn every penny of their revenue. However, I'd guess that they are the minority. Here's where I gather this assessment. I've witnessed many non-profit executives and their staffs push the organization's message using a combination of begging and guilt. It's pathetic to watch, but more importantly it often sabotages free enterprise and capitalism at the same time.

The old game of asking (aka: begging and pleading) for money is history. Smart, non-profits are quickly realizing that they must work harder than ever to show their relevance and reason for existence in a highly competitive market. The savvy ones are also realizing that they must become masters at transparency and continually be marketing their message in fresh and unique ways.

People are tired of sending donations blindly like they did when the economy was strong. They want and expect to see what type of impact their contribution is having directly on the front lines. Instead of "the economy's so bad" pitch, talk about success stories, new ideas and unique ways the non-profit is changing lives for the better. People are aware of the challenges in life, and they're growing immune to the same worn out appeals.

Successful, self-made people and companies are frowned upon or looked down on if they don't give enough money, time and volunteers. I agree it's smart to give back and the right thing to do if you find a cause in which you truly believe. However, this is a personal choice and up to each person to decide. No one should ever feel an obligation or guilt toward giving. Charities must also realize that bashing business, of any kind, is not smart. In many charitable circles, there's a smug resentment towards business and self-made or "new" money. "Old money" is acceptable because it comes from established social circles and foundations.  Wake up: Not all business people are rich, greedy or stealing from the poor. Again, go back and reread the last chapter for clarification if you need a check up from the neck up.

The third area of mental influence and opinion shaping in the marketplace to be aware of is in the political arena. It's easy to pick on politicians. Their number one fear-based tactic is to divide and conquer. Stir up the population and create a fear or enemy in people's minds. Use the fear to raise money and pass more laws, but rarely offer up solutions to get rid of the problem. Keeping the problem around is smart for them, but bad for you. You must resist getting caught up in their fear games and soap operas, so you can avoid wasting valuable time on their agenda versus focusing on your own.

Many of them change their minds often and pander to the biggest lobbying group or donor who can help them get reelected. This is a given and everyone knows it. Enough said.

Now that you're aware of the three main fear peddlers and how to guard your mind from their tactics and tendencies, let's examine the importance of persistence and focus in an age of instant digital gratification and massive distraction.

## CHAPTER 5:

# The Lost Art of Persistence

*"Perseverance separates the successful entrepreneurs
from the nonsuccessful ones."*
-Steve Jobs

BACK IN MAY 2008, I HAD THE pleasure to meet and hear Jeff Bezos, founder of online giant Amazon.com, speak at Book Expo America in Los Angeles. I was there to meet with my publisher and network. Bezos was making his first appearance in eight years to pitch the electronic book reader Kindle, and his presentation to a packed house was compelling and highly persuasive.

In his keynote address, he mentioned the many struggles he faced in the early days of selling his idea and the massive rejection and disdain by private investors and bankers for his idea of selling books online. They thought he was nuts. In his mind he believed 100% in his vision and nothing would stop him. We're all lucky today that he was a very persistent man. His company has turned the book publishing industry upside down and its impressive level of sales is rivaled by few businesses in the marketplace.

The highlight of his LA keynote speech was when he made a direct comment about the power of persistence and believing in your dream despite what others say or think. It was so powerful and timely that I now share it with every live group to which I speak.

**"Sometimes you have to be willing to be misunderstood."**

Please go back and slowly read that statement again. What an incredible idea. As soon as he said it, I stopped in my tracks and quickly realized that this was a common characteristic in high achievers. A simple piece of advice, but absolutely brilliant! I also have a rule: when a billionaire speaks, Tony stops whatever he's doing and listens. Bezos is right on with this advice.

As you promote your vision to others, be prepared for ridicule and rejection. I'm not trying to scare you, but prepare you for battle. Rejection is the breakfast of champions; you must conquer it daily to achieve success. For example, I can remember selling telephone services in my 20s and the massive amount of rejection I encountered in my first few years in the business. It was a strange paradox. Everybody needed what I was offering, but no one initially wanted to talk about it. To stay sane and motivated, I had a mental mantra that served my sales agents and me well the first couple of years when dealing with skeptical prospects. Here it is: *The thousands of nos will equal a few hundred yeses which can equal a fortune.*

In the sales profession, the ability to stay on track and follow up is another key to massive success. Here are some incredible statistics I uncovered a couple of years ago to help validate my point.

48% of sales people never follow up with a prospect
25% of sales people make a second contact and stop
12% of sales people only make three contacts and stop
Only 10% of sales people make more than three contacts
2% of sales are made on the first contact
3% of sales are made on the second contact

CHAPTER 5: **The Lost Art of Persistence** 41

5% of sales are made on the third contact
10% of sales are made on the fourth contact
80% of sales are made on the fifth to twelfth contact

*Tony note: If you'd like a handy free postcard that has these statistics to keep in your planner or near your desk, please drop me an email, Tony@MindCaptureGroup. com, with the Subject Line: Sales Statistics, and we'll mail it to you.*

Now, I'm not advocating that you waste time, but I can say that knowing your numbers and improving upon them constantly in any business is a major key to long-term success. Luckily, I realized, as I shared in my first *Mind Capture* book, getting good at marketing and studying the mindset and habits of other champions was the key to increasing sales and keeping a positive mindset, despite what prospects told me. I learned to never take a "no" personally. Top sales people live and breathe this simple, yet powerful advice.

### A Lesson From The Woods of Michigan

Being from the great state of Michigan and growing up in the country, my early years consisted of such fun jobs as picking blueberries and cutting wood with my stepfather and brothers. I have to admit that, at the time, I despised both jobs, but they did teach me the value of hard, physical labor.

It was simple. If we wanted the house kept warm over the winter, we cut and stacked wood in the fall. Humans have been doing this for thousands of years. If there's one valuable tip that I learned from chopping wood it's that you never let the first swing dictate your results. If you aren't persistent and swing the axe several times, you won't make a breakthrough. I find it fascinating that life is similar to cutting wood. Most people when they do finally muster up enough courage to pursue a dream or key goal take a few whacks at it, and often give up after a few rejections or challenges. They quit way too soon and fall back into the slacker club of excuses and regret.

Here's the biggest challenge facing most people today in relation to pursuing their dreams and passion. In an age of "instant everything" and the Internet, success rarely happens overnight. Most of the mega successful people I associate with have worked for years and through multiple setbacks to achieve their ultimate objectives. It also doesn't help that we've increasingly become a "lotto" mentality society. I firmly believe that the term "get-rich-quick" is a bold faced lie. There are the occasional needles in the haystack that pull it off, but keeping and sustaining success for the long-haul is an entirely different story.

True champions know they'll have to put the practice in like a top athlete and stretch much further than they ever thought possible if they really want to hit the goals they seek. New habits, associations and disciplines will be required. The classic quote from business philosopher Jim Rohn sums it up best:

*"No one can do your pushups for you."*

Far too many people wing it, give up or have no road map consisting of successful books, mentors and the proper mindset to guide and push them to discover and go after their inner genius. I never once found a class in my high school or college titled: **Goalsetting and Success 101**. Far too many of our schools teach people book skills and completely skip the life skills component. What a tragedy. We have millions of high school and college graduates trying to enter the work force with lots of book skills but little if any success mindset skills. They go into the employment game with a severe disadvantage right out of the gate. I sometimes forget that I was blessed to not only have the ability to pursue a college degree but also become exposed to two things even more beneficial along the way: mentors and personal development.

### Expect 'No' at First, But Press On

Here's another dose of the obvious that most people miss. People are conditioned to hear and say "no." In a perfect world, prospects would always get excited and say "yes" to our ideas but that's not the case. One of the biggest obstacles I encounter when training sales reps and business owners is how to handle rejection and the word "no" from a prospect. Many give up when they get the brush off or hear the first "no" when they should be thinking that the prospecting process has often just begun.

I've never known the word "no" to cause death, so why are people so afraid of hearing it? We all dislike rejection, but getting used to hearing it and moving beyond it is an essential trait of high achievers. There are a multitude of legendary success stories that exemplify the power of persistence and overcoming hundreds if not thousands of "nos" in pursuit of success.

A great example is fellow author and success master Jack Canfield of the wildly successful *Chicken Soup for the Soul*® publishing empire. Back in the early 1990s he and fellow co-author Mark Victor Hansen were turned down more than 140 times by publishers before finally landing a publishing contract. That's a whole lot of rejection, but in the end millions of happy readers have said "yes" to their message. What if they had given up at the 80th, 97th or 120th "no"? Most authors would have quit. Canfield and Hansen's tenacity and vision serve as a powerful lesson that anything is possible if you're persistent and look beyond rejection.

*Tony Note: At the end of the book, you'll find a special offer to download and listen to my recorded interview with Jack Canfield at no cost as a special thank you for purchasing this book.*

Our society as a whole dislikes sales and marketing. Here's the brutal truth that if you're new to personal development, you must quickly grasp and understand:

## EVERYONE IN SOCIETY IS IN THE SELLING BUSINESS

In the second *Mind Capture* book, I chronicled and explained the reasons everyone's in sales these days. I highlighted three unique professions that are showing up in my live audiences with much more frequency the last few years. They include ministers, accountants and lawyers. Sounds like the set up for a joke, but it's not a laughing matter. I've asked many of them at my programs what the attraction was to attend a sales and marketing driven program, and without hesitation they tell me that this is a skill they need to get better at. Do not be fooled. Everyone has an agenda, a goal or a plan. To have any shot at accomplishing it, they'll have to sell it to someone else.

The sales and marketing industries have been unfairly attacked and stereotyped by many within the media, political circles and academic circles. I find it to be extremely hypocritical that these three sectors of society are living by the motto of "do as I say, not as I do." If you're truly passionate about your goals, understand that many people will not roll out the welcome wagon to greet you. As a matter of fact, a classic quote sums it up best:

*"The higher up the ladder you go, the bigger*
*the bullseye on your back."*

My interpretation of this quote, based on my own personal life journey, is that this quote is right on. As you achieve more success, be prepared to encounter jealousy and envy from peers, associates and competitors. It will appear. It's how you battle through it and stay on course that matters most. How will you handle the fear and doubt that will also try its best to move in and play games with your mind? We'll examine a variety of ways to manage and overcome it.

Like the sales statistics I shared earlier in this chapter, most sales reps miss out on opportunities because they quit too soon or never circle back and follow up with a prospect. As we'll discuss in greater detail in the second half of this book, I'm a big believer that fortune is in the follow up.

### Five Years of Patient Follow Up = A Five Figure Payday

To demonstrate the power of persistence and good follow up, I'll share with you a recent success story to help inspire you and prove my point. Having spent nine years in the telecom industry of the go-go 1990s, I came across intense competition and learned a ton along the way about not only sales, persuasion and marketing, but also what the best companies did to be successful.

When I left the industry just weeks after 9/11, I stayed in touch with many of my former coworkers and some of the competitors I respected. After a short hiatus, I was hired by a former telecom competitor in 2004 to do a local sales training session for their troops based on my knowledge, history and expertise. The training was extremely well received, and I began to receive referrals within the region based on the results we had achieved. I was certain we'd be able to help even more people within this big organization.

Fast forward through the next five years and at least 25 follow up communications with various people in this organization, and finally a big breakthrough in April 2009. I invited the VP of Sales to see me speak at a book tour related event in Wisconsin that was literally three blocks from his office. He not only showed up, but he also brought along the director of their annual sales conference. Two months later and two more meetings, I received the "congratulations" phone call that I'd be their keynote speaker at their national sales conference. When I hung up the phone, I couldn't help but smile. Once again, persistence had paid off in a big way. The five figure check was great, but more importantly, I was able to help their entire sales force in one fell swoop.

While not everyone you engage or seek to serve will require this much follow up or patience, I encourage you to not give up too soon with prospects and former clients. This is a common mistake most people make and it costs them lots of profits and the opportunity to serve others. Many of my peers in the marketing industry can tell you that similar to follow up, the ability to continually stay in touch with clients to build a "back end" is where the true profit potential is contained within every business.

Another goal of this book is to share with you not only top-notch resources, but proven and concise ways to improve your own mindset to help you push on with bull headed intensity. Persistence and follow up are essential traits you must learn, practice, and make a daily habit on your path to achieving success and serving more people.

Now that we've looked at why persistence is important to your success, we'll explore why innovation and creativity are essential in your pursuit of achieving your goals.

## CHAPTER 6:
# Innovation Trumps Mediocrity

*"The economy stopped, but progress didn't."*
-Matt Hanlon

I'M ALWAYS AMAZED THAT WHEN we slow ourselves down and listen closely to others some of the most amazing insights can occur. The quote to start this chapter is a great kickoff for the next lesson and was recently given to me when I was having a cup of coffee with my friend Matt Hanlon, who's one of the sharpest sales executives I've ever met. We were fully engaged discussing the economy, and he summed up brilliantly in one simple sentence what he observed taking place. Luckily, I stopped him, grabbed a pen and paper, and now his wisdom lives on to be shared with others via this book.

I've had the honor to train his radio teams here in Michigan, and I can tell you that they're like Navy Seals in comparison to most sales organizations I work with. They're extremely sharp, well trained, action oriented, and know how to employ several smart tactics to assist them when selling in a difficult industry. Matt's ability to lead from the front and let them try unique ideas and innovate constantly is a key ingredient to their success.

You just never know when a great idea or insight will strike your mind. It happens to me often; many times when I least expect it. For example, I'll be in front of an audience sharing marketing strategies and someone will make a comment or ask a question. My mind comes up with something quickly and I blurt out a supporting idea or answer that not only floors the audience but yours truly. I'm not sure if it's a miracle or the adrenalin rush of creating ideas unscripted in front of a group, but it never ceases to amaze and inspire me.

I was in Montgomery, Alabama, last year doing a keynote presentation for a group of 200 business leaders from around the state when the genesis for this chapter was born. I was midway through my talk and on a roll about why great companies and their people always look to solve problems when I spouted out, *Innovation trumps mediocrity*. I stopped myself and offered a free book to the first person who emailed me the comment. This was an "aha moment" and I couldn't let this gem slip away. I was fortunate that a person in the session followed up with an email, as the quote now serves as the focal point for this chapter's message to help you rekindle the awesome power of your imagination.

Victim mentality and excuses are running rampant and kill the ability to innovate. Here's one of my mottos to help you avoid these two innovation destroyers and inspire you to make positive change a daily habit in your life:

### Step Up and Offer Solutions or Shut Up and Sit Back Down

Tony, that sounds offensive and mean spirited. Maybe. Frankly, I think it's what more people need to hear. Our society, media and government sadly reward and encourage people to make excuses, avoid responsibility and pass the buck to someone else. This is a fact. This offends many people because they know that deep down it's the truth, and often the truth is not what they want to accept or believe.

**Case in point:** One of the biggest myths still being pushed is the concept of economic security. In the last two years we've seen giants of industry reduced to ashes in lost jobs, equity and stature. I bet many of the so called leaders at these firms bought into a false sense of "security" and foolishly ignored the warning signs of changing market conditions.

Countless new ideas and solutions from employees and customers were likely ignored and stifled by a combination of politics and a sense of arrogance which has cost our economy dearly. I'm certain that many people in these firms knew trouble was brewing, but stayed on a sinking ship because they believed in "security" versus exiting on their own terms. So what's the lesson for each of us? It's not easy, but let me give you the reason each of us needs to learn and grow from this dark economic time.

## The World Needs <u>You</u> to Step Up and Take Action

No one can save you but yourself. You must reengage your talents, ideas, habits, knowledge base, associations and dreams to turn things around in your own life. The bailout mentality is a short term illusion that does not solve long-term problems. If we're to turn the economy around, it will require you to move past the status quo thinking of "security" to a new paradigm of trusting in your own God-given abilities and working on them relentlessly. My friend Patrick Snow describes this process as "creating your own destiny" and he's spot on with his assessment.

Great ideas and solutions are always present. The challenge for most of us is to capture them when they strike and act on them. There's no shortage of ideas. The world has millions of great ideas floating around looking for the right person to seize and mold them into physical form. The real challenge is a shortage of belief in the ideas and an even greater shortage of those who act on them.

**12 great ways to "Capture" the power of innovation and
take more positive action within your life:**

1.  Study and read in multiple disciplines
2.  Always maintain curiosity as to why things are the way they are
3.  Listen for problems in your market or industry and create or find ways to solve them
4.  Learn how great organizations get ahead and model their success within your business
5.  Always capture and record great ideas immediately when they strike by having a pen and paper ready
6.  Bounce new ideas off of key associates, customers and those you network with online and offline
7.  Circulate by attending new events
8.  Hang around successful people and soak in their wisdom and ideas
9.  Make it a goal to implement one new idea into your business at least once a week
10. Get in better physical shape so you can cultivate more mental and physical energy
11. Ask questions and make it a goal to learn at least one new thing per day that advances your goals
12. Build leisure and goof off time within your busy schedule as many of the best ideas will hit you when you least expect it and are in a relaxed state of mind

It's obvious to me, based on my own daily experiences and readings, that high achievers all share a common bond. We all have a strong curiosity toward life, and a passion for uncovering why things are the way they are and what we can do to change or improve upon them. The status quo drives us nuts. Call it rebellion, impatience, maybe even arrogance in some people's minds, but it's often present in those who are living fully engaged and on a mission. It's as if most of the world is stuck in slow motion wasting valuable minutes, hours and days on details of little significance in the grand scheme of things.

### The Lesson from Children

The sense of possibility and curiosity is natural in children, but as we age and negative societal programming kicks into high gear, most people lose this powerful talent. I'm amazed at how many people sabotage their greatness, genius and dreams out of fear-based thinking or based on what others say they can or can't do. Is it any wonder today that we have so many book-smart people who can't find a job or are afraid to finally start a business they've always wanted to pursue? In addition, the #1 challenge most adults have when creating positive, new beliefs and habits is getting rid of the years of bad programming and influence clouding their mind and tempting them to stay "comfortable" versus taking a risk to improve their lives.

Many institutions reward "play-it-safe" mentality and years of service instead of results and creativity. As I noted earlier in the book, the big three societal influencers consisting of the media, your associations and the marketplace do have a MAJOR influence, primarily negative and toxic if you don't monitor them carefully, on your ability to achieve success.

There is good news. One group in particular seems to be immune to the mental illness of negative societal programming and they have a major piece of wisdom that we can all learn from. Yes, I'm alluding to children, and I need you to stay with me for the gem they teach us about innovation and living life fully engaged and on purpose. But first, I need to share with you a powerful, true-life story that happened a couple of summers ago.

### Braydon's Question

Our home is a busy place. Three kids, three dogs and four cats should give you a clue. There's always movement, excitement and action. It was a beautiful June Saturday morning in Michigan last year and my son, Braydon, and I were heading through the garage to play in the front yard. I noted that we had a guest sneak out the back door with us. His name: Jake, our "middle" chocolate lab. As he bolted down the driveway, my son and I went in hot pursuit and captured him. As we let him back in the garage, I closed the door and turned around towards my son when he asked me this question:

*"Dad, how come Jake doesn't wear clothes like we do?"*

To say that I was speechless is a massive understatement. Shocked and dumbfounded is a more accurate description. My mind raced to try and come up with an answer to this strange, yet brilliant question and after a couple of seconds, the first thing I uttered from my mouth was, "Ask your mother." I tried not to laugh out loud as it was initially a cute "father-son" moment, but I soon realized it was much, much more than that. As we played, I kept reverting back to my son's question in my mind and why it was so simple, yet powerful when it hit me like a sledgehammer. Kids have no paradigms or rules which govern their creativity.

Here's the gem, as promised, that kids can teach each of us about the power of innovation: They look at life and even everyday things with **fresh eyes**. They don't bring any baggage to the table. Life is new, and they question what we as adults often assume and take for granted. Nothing is mundane to them. Between the ages of two to seven, everything's new and a child's ability to learn and innovate is unmatched.

So what happens as we grow up? Many of us lose our ability to create, question, and innovate. We replace this wonderful talent with a wide variety of left brain skills, logic and fear-based programming. Problem solving and the ability to think for ourselves are often sacrificed for the sake of being a team player or to not offend anyone. Creativity becomes snuffed out, quickly replaced by rules, structure and other socially acceptable programming.

Now, we'll move into the realm of money and why it's important to create your own stimulus plan now versus ever waiting for someone to hand it to you for free. That's called lotto mentality, and again it's a big illusion being pushed from the fear peddlers to trick, suppress and distract your mind from pursuing your own inner genius.

# SECTION 2:

## MIND Matters – Strategies To Awaken The NEW You

## CHAPTER 7

# Create Your Own Stimulus Plan

*"The more you make your own mind-conscious and subconscious-of just how much affluence there is, just how much money is moving around, the more easily you will attract wealth."*
-Dan Kennedy

WE'VE BEEN WORKING PRIMARILY on the mind in the first several chapters of this book, and now it's time to focus on the physical realm of productive strategies for taking action on a consistent basis.

We'll explore three time-tested, battle-ready techniques for creating your own stimulus plan. They include:

1. Systems to monetize your genius via multiple streams of income
2. The power of option-based thinking
3. Using momentum as your friend and ally

In respect of time, I'm going to recommend additional resources for further study and application in this section that are the best I've discovered and used within my own life and business for you to read and apply towards this book's message and teachings. I'll open the door, get you started, and also allow other sages to push you through it. They will help to complement and build on the strategies I'm advocating as they relate to creating your own stimulus plan.

### #1. The Power of Systems and Multiple Streams of Income

In the Fall of 2008 in Orlando, Florida, I had the honor to share the stage at an event with two of my business heroes, Les Brown and Michael Gerber, at a large chamber of commerce function. Talk about not only a wonderful event, but I was also given the tall order of speaking directly after each of them on the program agenda. No pressure, right! Not many speakers can say that they've shared the stage with both of these guys, yet alone had to follow them on the same agenda. While Les is the great motivator, Gerber is the systems guru. His book, *The E-Myth*, is one of my top ten favorite business books and is a required read for anyone serious about not just being in business, but staying in business for the long haul.

Having recently reached year five in business with my own company, I can tell you that setting up systems is absolutely essential to your success. Without systems, you will bump into a capacity and time barrier that will limit your ability to serve more people, expand your inner genius and build long-term wealth.

I will not attempt to expound on the power of systems here, Michael's book does it marvelously well, but I do want to examine why you need systems in your life to build multiple streams of income and your own stimulus plan. The biggest fallacy many people are still buying into is that you can rely on one source of income. Sadly, many in the media, academia, unions, and the government are pushing this antiquated advice in the age of global competition and massive web-based competition. I'll spare you the history lesson as to why this is still being packaged and sold, as the goal here is to focus on what we can directly change. Relying on one source of income is extremely dangerous for many reasons including:

- It limits your ability to make adjustments if you lose your job, main source of income or a key customer
- It stifles your ability to take risks and often conditions you to "play it-safe"
- The cost of living is increasing faster than the typical pay increase
- You're up against the timeless advice which says not to put all of your eggs in one basket

As we've already discussed previously, counting on job security is a dangerous idea not only to your mental space but often, as we've seen especially in the last two years in the global economy, to your financial future as well. I strongly advocate that you continue to leverage and build your other skills, hobbies, and passions to discover ways to monetize them for additional income. Please remember that we're all unique and have different talents and varied life experiences to draw upon for wisdom. One of my early mentors was fond of a simple, yet extremely wise, piece of advice that I'll share with you now:

*"What you take for granted, others will pay for."*

I have never forgotten this simple piece of advice, and it has served me and those I share it with very well. In a complex world, we often forget the simple things that make a major impact if we're open to really trust and believe in ourselves.

Here's the big secret to making money and creating multiple streams of income in your life that's so obvious that most people refuse to believe or downplay its power when they first hear it:

**Find a problem(s) in the marketplace and create or seek out a way for people to pay you for the solution.**

*Tony, is it really that easy? Are you kidding me?* While it will take some homework and inner reflection based on your own skills and new ones you'll need to acquire, I've seen time and time again that the most successful companies are those that solve the greatest number of problems. I know it's not sexy or mysterious, and frankly, the danger lies in its simplicity. Why do we humans always make things so much more complex than they really are? One possible answer is that many people have a deeply seeded belief that common sense is a gimmick or untrue.

Again, in the age of information overload, the timeless wisdom of Albert Einstein comes to mind with his belief that genius is making the complex simple. I couldn't agree with him more as it relates to the ability to solve problems today. Here's a quick 'Top 10' list of ongoing action items to guide you and refer back to when pursuing multiple streams of income:

1. Seek out wise mentors who are successful in your area of interest
2. Realize that you must become and stay a life-long learner
3. Set up and find a good banking partner, insurance pro and CPA in advance
4. Understand that strong sales and marketing skills are required for long-term success
5. Look for logical synergies within your income streams to leverage time, contacts and cross-selling opportunities
6. Continually work on building systems within your business to free up more time to pursue bigger and better opportunities – delegate and expand **or** do-it-all and die trying
7. Stay passionate about your mission or you'll find the temptation to quit a strong urge when you encounter challenges and rejection
8. Build in flexibility within your goals so you can make adjustments to your business based on new information and changes in the market that you can use to your marketing advantage
9. Cash is king, so manage it wisely (and don't run out of it!)
10. Listen to your best customers to find new product and service offerings that you can provide to add more value to their experience and profits to your bottom line

*Don't ask what the world needs.*
*Ask what makes you come alive, and go do it.*
*Because what the world needs is people who have come alive.*
-Howard Thurman

## #2. The Power of Option-Based Thinking

I'm amazed when watching a Disney movie or TV show with our children how many times the young hero or main character finds him or herself in a jam and magically comes up with a new idea to solve the problem. It's like the old TV show, MacGyver, where the main character always ended up trapped by the bad guys and quickly figured out a way to set himself free and manage to capture the bad guys, too. What's the common thread here? It's simple: persistence and what I call option-based thinking.

Unfortunately, many people let a combination of ignorance and bad mental habits destroy or cloud their ability to solve problems via option-based thinking. Children have an advantage as their inner genius and right-brained skills of creativity are strong and in full swing. As we age, many of us lose this inner genius based on habits, belief structures and the negative or misguided opinions of others who seek to suppress and condition us to play it safe.

It's also a very real challenge and concern that our attention spans are getting shorter and shorter. As we race into the age of real-time communication, our growing appetite for "instant everything" is being catered to by search engine technology and staggering amounts of choice delivered via local and web-based competition. With this in mind, many people have lost or buried their ability to sit down and create different options and solutions when confronted with a problem. Damn it, if we can't find a solution on Google in under 5 minutes, we throw our hands up in the air and either give up or move onto the next distraction. Some of you are laughing right now because you know that I've just described you.

### Changing Market Conditions Requires Changing Beliefs

The shift is happening right before our eyes and if you're a student of history, this won't come as a surprise. In the early 1900s many people in the US were self-employed or worked in agriculture. When the industrial revolution happened, many people gave this up and moved to the cities to work in the emerging industrial economy. Many traded self-reliance for a paycheck, guaranteed employment, and retirement benefits upon a completed working career with one central employer or industry. Whoa. This model is ancient history, but a vast majority of people still believe that this is an option. Snap out of it. Let me run smelling salts under your nose. This old paradigm and economic model has been steadily decaying away the last 25 years, and it's now speeding up with ferocious intensity.

### The Entrepreneur Strikes Back

Similar to the title of the classic second Star Wars movie subtitled, *The Empire Strikes Back*, I believe a new era is rushing in at breakneck speed: The age of the entrepreneur. People are quickly waking up to the fact that the days of working for someone else exclusively are not only outdated, but dangerous to your income. Once again, people are breaking out of the trap known as denial and beginning to question the status quo. This is a good thing. Without change there's no progress. Let's look at how you can create the change you desire within your life versus the illusion and lie that waiting around for someone else to deliver it to you is a viable or smart option.

Having the ability to think with multiple options in mind is not only a powerful skill to master, but a requirement to successfully navigate the changing economic waters. Safety within any business is having multiple revenue centers to prosper during boom times and maintain during pullbacks and recessions. Why is it then that most people do not create a plan b, c or d when they approach their lives? I'm not advocating being wimpy and giving up because you have easier options available at the first sign of trouble. What I am stressing is that you need to think of best case and worst case scenarios and map out a plan of options to guide you when confronted with either scenario.

We have very few people today that think like this. This is a bold observation. The proof is all around you that far too many people have no idea of how to react when confronted with change or a tight economy. For example, our government and business sectors are loaded with far too many excuse makers who haven't employed or even know how to act on option-based thinking.

*"In a time of peace, prepare for war."*

What's up with all the summits, hearings, panels and forums lately in Washington, DC? Having these meetings with the media tripping over themselves with commentary on the grand ideas and good speeches is one thing, but taking decisive, positive action appears to be another story altogether. Like a drunken sailor on an all night party binge, the hangover will hit the next day after the music stops. It's usually not a pretty sight and the recovery is painful. Similarly, our economy is having a hangover that was built on many assumptions that are far too numerous to warrant space in this book. One obvious cause for the current meltdown is the fact that little thought was given to future planning and using option-based thinking in case the U.S. economy slowed down.

*"When one door closes, another opens."*

So how do you build a powerful option-based mindset? There are many, but here are three of the best ways I've discovered and use myself:

**#1. Think on paper.** It's amazing what happens when you capture and crystallize ideas on paper. Not only does it let you map out and list ideas and strategies, but more importantly, the odds increase dramatically that you'll review and implement what you've written. I always carry paper and pen as ideas, tips and solutions to challenges and opportunities hit my mind all day long when I often least expect them. Never, ever, ever trust your memory. When the iron is hot, do not risk losing a great idea or solution because you forget to capture it and record it on paper.

I also encourage you to keep a written journal containing your top one-year goals, business ideas, and other sources of wisdom as my friend and fellow speaker Dave Sheffield describes as "mental floss" to keep your mind clean and focused on your highest priorities. In the next few chapters, we'll discuss other action items you'll want to plug in and add to your written journal for continual reference and application in your life. Thinking on paper and keeping the best nuggets in one central journal are also habits of many high achievers to model and use for your own life.

One of the more powerful books I've ever read that helps explain why our mind is a powerful tool when trained is *Psycho Cybernetics* by the late Maxwell Maltz. He explains why the servo mechanism within our minds can work either for or against us, and the book details how to reprogram it like a new software application to make it our ally.

**#2. Do your homework.** Study and glean wisdom from those who've been confronted with challenges you face via books, masterminding with other sharp people, doing research online, and asking smart questions of those you can trust. In the age of instant search, the world is at your fingertips. It's frustrating when I work with a business owner, marketing team, or sales group that's having a business challenge and I ask if they've done any research to find possible solutions to the problem, and they sheepishly say "no," or "we've been too busy." These are nothing more than excuses and laziness with their business priorities because they've done little if any homework beyond a 5-10 minute search on Google or maybe asking one or two other colleagues for advice.

Doing due diligence on your own destiny and business is an ongoing process. Look around you at how many businesses have struggled out of ignorance and dated assumptions. Market conditions changed, knowledge increased, the competition improved, and they chose to deny and ignore it. Far too many people skip the homework step and rely on bad advice which costs them a fortune in more ways than they will ever know.

For example, in my home state of Michigan, denial and basing reality on outdated ways of doing business is a big, big problem that is crushing our state's ability to compete in the global economy. Far too many people in various realms of supposed leadership long for the "good old days," and it has cost many of my neighbors and businesses a heavy toll in lost jobs, opportunities and diminished profits. Solution-based thinking is foreign to many of them. Ignorance is taking its toll.

The central paradox in the digital age of communication is that most people are wired to dislike change and "settle" into habits that often work against their true potential. Many of their engrained habits are holding them back. In addition, ignoring new information, updates and breakthroughs in their field is a recipe for disaster and missed opportunities. I have faith and confidence that you believe this, otherwise you wouldn't have invested your time and money reading these words. Research shows that most people buy books and never get beyond the first 20 pages. What a shame indeed.

### #3. Using momentum as your best friend and ally

The world rewards action. Until you're in motion, nothing will change. Yes, another case of the obvious. I've lost track of how many people I've met who still have their dreams, ideas, inventions and solutions buried in their minds or stuck on a shelf in their home or office collecting dust. They are imprisoned in a mental room of their own design, with four walls they've constructed which go by the names of: procrastination, doubt, fear and security. How do I know this? I've had to escape from this room myself and strive each day to rarely visit it or hang out there very long. In the short term, it's a very comfortable room and that's the immense danger it possesses. In an instant world, success is rarely achieved quickly. Yes, there are shortcuts, but you still have to put in the necessary work and refine your skills on a continual basis.

Here's a powerful quote I heard many years ago at a live seminar that Captured my Mind and changed my destiny in relation to the power that momentum has on our lives:

*"You don't have to get it right. You just have to get it going."*

I'll tell you upfront that this is simple, yet powerful advice if you look beyond the initial perception that it encourages sloppy or harmful behavior. In my opinion, this quote encompasses three big concepts:

1. Get busy
2. Get your plan, idea or goals into action sooner rather than later
3. Get momentum on your side and make adjustments along the way

So what's one of the smartest ways to use momentum in your life? Cultivate and build the habit of creating deadlines tied to the biggest goals within your life. The best way to do this is by setting daily, weekly, monthly and yearly deadlines and working each day to hit certain ones, but also move the ball forward to get you closer to achieving bigger deadlines. I know it's not sexy, but it's essential to do because it works.

*"Motion beats meditation."*
-Gary Halbert

As you move into action and begin knocking off key activities linked to the deadlines you've set, you'll gain confidence and momentum to pick up the pace and stay on track. Once you get in this positive habit of hitting deadlines, momentum and velocity will intensify. This is not an accident. In fact this book is an example of this concept. It's a series of goals, deadlines and action steps that had to be completed using momentum in order for the book to be written, edited and published.

**Action steps:** Take a few minutes and list on the next page three things in your own life that you've wanted to do the last few years that could dramatically improve your life, but that you've put off time and time again. In addition, list below each item one immediate thing you can do today to employ momentum and get the ball rolling toward achieving it. I also ask that you write down a deadline and one resource you can call upon to set in motion the idea immediately to aid you in completion of each goal.

1.      Delayed Goal:_____

        Action Today:
        Deadline Date:
        Resource to Help:

2.      Delayed Goal:_____

        Action Today:
        Deadline Date:
        Resource to Help:

3.      Delayed Goal:_____

        Action Today:
        Deadline Date:
        Resource to Help:

By doing the above action exercise, you're also setting into motion the two option-based thinking strategies of thinking on paper and doing your homework. There's still more to do of course, but these are two critically important first steps that many people neglect to do in the early stages that often cost them both time and missed opportunities.

> *"...ideas are about the cheapest of all commodities...*
> *But the supply of men who can execute ideas and*
> *make money out of them is pitifully small."*
> -Bruce Barton

Now that you've taken aggressive action steps to get positive momentum working for you, it's time to explore the importance that other people will play on your path to finding and achieving your inner genius.

# CHAPTER 8:

# People Mastery

*"So the only way to influence the other fellow is
to talk about what he wants and show him how to get it."*
-Dale Carnegie

SEND ME AN EMAIL, TEXT ME, FOLLOW ME on Twitter network with me on LinkedIn or friend request me on Facebook are common sayings in the digital age. Your ability to persuade and influence others with your ideas, goals and passion is one of the most important skills to master. You may have the greatest product, service or idea but if the other person can't connect with you, you're in trouble. Here are the big three challenges we must all confront and deal with as it relates to face-to-face communication in the Internet age:

1. Shortened attention spans
2. Heavy reliance on digital communication versus talking or meeting with each other face-to-face
3. Standing out or achieving what I call 'Mind Capture'

The old adage *"Out of sight, out of mind"* is timeless and accurate. Not only do you have to be visible in the online space, but also in the physical realm. In this chapter, we'll explore several powerful ways to sharpen your people skills while I reveal many great resources to accelerate your success. Some are timeless, while others you may be hearing about for the first time. Yes, at times this lost art may seem "old school" but you'll soon discover it is critical to get and stay good at.

I've noticed something the last few years that's both aggravating and scary when dealing with people in not only business but society: many people allow technology to run them ragged. Like drug addicts painfully looking for their next fix, most people will willingly and without reservation allow just about anybody to find and interrupt them. Then they complain to others why they feel overwhelmed and can't get anything done. This "always on" mentality is killing not only productivity but most people's ability to communicate effectively in a face-to-face situation. The proper **balance** of managing input and access is required and should be continually monitored.

In this chapter we'll explore:

- World-class networking skills that high achievers use to get ahead and stay ahead
- Why getting face-to-face time is critical to your success
- Seven valuable ways to connect with others

### In The Game of Business, Realize That Whom You Know Is Often More Important Than What You Know

Success to me is pursuing your passion or inner genius and finding a way to get paid for it. If you have great ideas and end up broke, not only do your ideas serve the few if anyone else, but they cripple you at the same time. The pursuit of success is never a solo journey. Your ability to persuade others is a central building block, but even more important is the ability to attract quality people along the way. I've learned recently that most people do not grasp how much more effective networking is compared to cold marketing. Yes, a flash of the obvious for some of you, but let me explain in greater detail.

The cost of cold marketing continues to escalate, and reaching people is even more challenging. I'm not saying to stop your prospecting efforts. I still use and teach clients many proven direct response lead generation and follow up strategies; however, I am suggesting that most people are not well versed in how to network like a champion. They often downplay its power and potential because they treat it with little respect and have never studied what top networkers do to achieve quantum breakthroughs in reaching their goals faster.

Here are two quick tips to help you network more effectively online and offline:

1.  Have a great 15-second commercial
2.  Follow up quickly or risk being forgotten

It's stunning how many people I meet in a given week when I'm speaking or traveling that are unmemorable. Not that they're bad people, but their lack of creativity and charisma often leaves me unimpressed. They open their mouths to tell me what they do, but only a handful capture and really grab my attention. Each day, most people continue to miss networking opportunities to present themselves like pros and pick up valuable contacts. This is based on a combination of laziness, fear and lack of creativity. Let's discuss how you can join the elite group of people who are masters of this skill.

The term "elevator pitch" refers to someone's ability to pitch, tell or answer the question "what do you do?" from a complete stranger in a succinct and memorable way. These encounters happen millions of times a day around the world, and I'd wager that 95% of these responses are done poorly, thus many potential opportunities are wasted. In a tightening economy, I'm a big believer that refining your sales processes and systems is a good thing to do especially when it comes to networking. Regardless of whether your marketing budget's the same as last year or has been cut, great networking skills are a powerful and low cost ally to have in your arsenal.

I must confess that my elevator pitch for many years was uninspiring and unmemorable. It was boring and I often winged it. You want to test, practice and own your commercial once you've come up with one that captures people's minds. Here are the two commercials I currently use that work very effectively for my company:

1.  *I perform marketing exorcisms*
2.  *I'm in town today to perform a marketing intervention*

Let me share with you a few strategies and examples to modify and consider for your own business to help you create a great 15-second commercial that produces both contacts and business:

**Make it catchy or play off a hot topic or trend.**
Example: "Do you know how people are talking a lot these days about the economy? I show them how to _____ even when they think it's not possible."

**Share a recent success story of interest.**
Example: "We recently helped a business here in town by showing them _____."

**Use shock value to get your prospect to really think.**
Example: "What if you ignored _____ and it became a major problem you could have easily avoided?"

**Explain a common problem and how you can solve it.**
Example: "You know how people always seem to complain about _____? Well, we know how to solve this challenge quickly and easily."

## The Power of Fewer, Deeper Relationships In Your Networking Efforts

In the last two years, I've had the honor to meet lots of great new people via my travels, seminars and book-related events. One person in particular who really stands out to me as the master of networking is my friend and fellow entrepreneur Dave Stech. Forget the "six-degrees of separation" theory. He networks at a deeper level than anyone else I've ever met.

Dave teaches and has trademarked the term *The Power of Six*™. It appears simple on the surface, yet very potent when applied. His premise is that you should seek out and establish deeper, stronger business relationships with six key people who are just as sharp if not better than you in other areas of your life and business. Instead of networking with lots of people at the surface level, change your approach to think of quality versus quantity in the networking process to achieve breakthroughs much faster and in a far more focused manner.

In his forthcoming book on the topic, Dave breaks down in greater detail what you need to look for in your six people and how you can leverage and serve one another versus going at it alone. I'm a believer in his strategy and also recommend that you still seek out select networking groups and key visibility opportunities in which you and your company can participate.

## Face-to-Face Selling is Alive and Well

I can't help but shake my head and chuckle at people who keep canceling meetings and conventions or who skip their industry trade shows based on fear and cutbacks in budgets. Not only is this the wrong thing to do when members are counting on getting value for their association dues, but while others stay at home with their list or reasons (excuses) for not attending, I'm hopping planes to meet with people in the flesh.

I'll be very direct with you now about what you should strongly consider if your employer cuts back on travel and expenses. If your company won't pay for you to go to a key meeting or convention, dig into your own pockets and pay for it yourself. If it's that important, quit whining and invest in yourself and your customers and pick up new contacts and business. In both of my prior careers, I **always** invested a healthy sum from my commission checks in books, seminars and travel that my employer would not cover. Hmm? *If I invest in myself, it seems that everybody wins. My customers, business, family and community all gain and benefit from this action.*

Following are five Mind Capture tips to get valuable face-to-face time with other people:

1.  Promise speed
2.  Use block scheduling
3.  Employ a guarantee or gift with appointment
4.  Get on a plane
5.  Join and participate in key trade and association groups

Let's take a quick look at these five tips and the logic behind each one.

**#1. Promise speed.** Everyone's busy these days and the quickest way to lose someone is to imply that what you have to offer or discuss will take up a lot of their time. I often get super busy people to pay attention because I tell them upfront that we're both busy, and I only need a few minutes. If I sense that we're connecting, I ask permission for more time and often get it. It works like a charm and it disarms their fear that I'll waste a lot of their time. I know I'm appreciative as well when people respect my time and get to the point sooner rather than later.

If you get stuck in proverbial "voicemail hell" when trying to connect with a busy person, have no fear, as there are many ways to solve this problem. In the first *Mind Capture* book, I reveal several proven ways to leave a powerful message and use targeted and unique direct mailings to get busy decision makers to take notice and accept your call or get back to you when you leave an engaging voicemail message.

**#2. Use block scheduling.** I learned this valuable tip from my central mentor, Dan Kennedy, and it flat out works. When I travel, I do my best to fully leverage and maximize the trip. I call key prospects and groups in the area where I'll be working to let them know the specific date(s) I'll be in town and open times available to schedule meetings. This is a great opportunity for me to give them an invitation to see me speak at my engagement or a chance to get together before or after an already scheduled meeting. This gives both parties leverage: I come to them well-prepared, and they know I'm offering a legitimate chance to meet face-to-face versus other speakers who only do a phone call or email.

I also use and recommend this strategy because it gives you a legitimate reason to connect with someone on their home turf when you'll already be in town anyway. People still often like to meet someone in person to get a feel for who they are before they will consider doing any business. I can tell you that over the last few years alone, this tip has generated countless dollars in new business with prospective individual and group clients who have hired me direct or booked me to speak after an in-person meeting or after attending one of my live speaking programs.

**#3. Employ a guarantee or gift with appointment.** This goes back to tip number one in regard to the fact that people are very skeptical in general and do not want their time wasted. I believe that getting face time in the digital age will remain the biggest challenge for everyone in marketing. With this in mind, a great way to get someone off the fence and in motion is to offer something of value for a chance to meet by boldly backing up your request with a guarantee to set them at ease. I'm not advocating bribery here, but simply a creative way to get a meeting scheduled when other strategies to meet have met resistance or delay.

You may offer a special report, book or a small donation to a favorite charity to peak curiosity and to imply how serious you are about your idea. One of my favorite strategies is to offer a free copy of my latest book and recent audio interviews on CD just for meeting with me. Prospects benefit from the timely and relevant information whether we decide to work together or not. I enjoy being able to reward and thank them for taking the time to consider what I'm proposing.

**#4. Get on a plane.** You have to go to where the action is, and often to where the prospect or client calls home. Now, I'm all about saving time, and again, balance is required with this tip. I'm not paid by the airlines to put this in the book, but here's the point: If it's a big enough opportunity to gain face time and knock out other meetings via block scheduling, book your trip and fly in to meet people. Let the media scare away your competition from spending money on business travel. While they're at home often making futile attempts to reach decision makers, you'll be meeting and shaking hands with top prospects and cementing long-standing relationships.

For example, every year I attend a major trade group's convention in January. It's not so much to attend the show, but to set up important breakfast and lunch meetings with key decision makers that I know are all in town for the week. I can get more done in two days with face-to-face meetings than I could in a year of detailed and time draining follow up. Press the flesh to impress and get valuable face time!

**#5. Join and participate in key trade and association groups.** Yes, a simple strategy. But here's a quick and important tip that a lot of people overlook: Join one or two key associations where your top customers and referral partners congregate. Instead of only spending time in your own industry groups, go to where the best prospects are located and get busy. I'm baffled as to why more people don't budget dues and allocate sponsor dollars to allow for focused networking time in their marketing plans so they can be noticed and connect with the best prospects for their business.

I recently interviewed networking guru, Dr. Ivan Misner, founder of the massively successful referral organization BNI (Business Network International). In our interview, he mentioned that the top performers in many BNI chapters devote six to eight hours per week to focused and strategic networking– everything from attending their weekly chapter meeting, to chamber events and meeting with key clients and referral partners each week over coffee, breakfast or lunch to exchange ideas, contacts and helpful information. Yes, it's a serious commitment, but these people often get incredible results toward achieving their goals.

*Tony note: at the end of the book you'll see a special free offer to hear my interview with Dr. Misner as a special thank you for investing in this book!*

*"In everyone's life, at some time, our inner fire goes out.*
*It is then burst into flame by an encounter with another human being.*
*We should all be thankful for those people who rekindle the inner spirit."*
-Albert Schweitzer

### Seven Valuable Ways To Connect With Others

Consider this section as your short cut in the digital age on how to connect at a deeper level with every person you meet. The only two exceptions: Dream stealers and negative people whom you don't want around you anyway.

**#1. Listen, listen, listen.** Take an interest in others first and you'll be pleased with how much more receptive and friendly they'll be with you and your message. Use well thought-out questions, take mental and written notes, and seek out common areas of interest. The goal is to harmonize and build rapport first, and then tell them your idea or story. Remember: people care about themselves first, then you and your agenda. This is universal regardless of new communication tools or trends.

In an age of advertising overload and instant communication, when you take a serious interest in others they will feel appreciated and often share many valuable insights into what makes them tick. Look around you. Patient and focused listening is in short supply. People often let others interrupt and distract them via calls to their cell phone, emails and instant messaging. This severely hampers the ability to listen and truly focus in on the other person's words and body language. Poor listening skills cost people countless opportunities each day that they often miss because they hadn't been paying close attention and really listening to others.

**#2. Do your homework.** Why are people so lazy when it comes to this step? Millions of sales presentations start out with this painful question: *So, tell me about your business and how's it going?* Bad, bad, bad! This not only insults the prospect, but it shows a serious flaw that the person did not do his or her homework. In the age of Google, you can find a plethora of information in less than five minutes related to just about any company, person or industry. In the second *Mind Capture* book, I describe this as being Google-licous, and it's a smart way to find out key information pertaining to a prospect or customer.

Another powerful strategy when doing your homework is to seek out those who do business with a key contact or company that you're trying to make a connection with. Once you find them, call or email the key person to see if he or she can assist or give you insight on key decision makers and what makes the company click. Be quick, respectful, and also identify their needs to see if you might be of assistance to them now or down the line for being gracious enough to help and give you their valuable time. This has gotten infinitely easier with the web, new social media platforms such as Facebook and LinkedIn, and the ease of data available at little or no cost from online information providers such as InfoUSA or Hoovers.

**#3. Employ confidence and look sharp.** I'm going to make this short and sweet. If you have any problem speaking to groups, organizing your thoughts or selling yourself and your ideas, then I have two immediate resources for you: Toastmasters and Dale Carnegie training. These two groups have a track record of success that's undisputed. I would not be doing what I do today and at the level of mastery if it weren't for 12 years of membership in my local Toastmasters club. To get up in front of several hundred people at a time to engage and lead them for an hour or two is not a simple feat. This was made possible by giving hundreds of talks, getting continual feedback from respected peers and mentors and via intense study of the speaking business. Many people think it comes easy and is a gift that just comes naturally to some. This is completely false. Unfortunately, overnight success is a myth that's still being packaged and sold in the age of instant everything. Great communicators are made, not born.

Your ability to effectively communicate to individuals, groups, and committees is of primary importance. When you earn valuable time, especially face-to-face, you must quickly impress and demonstrate to others why your idea or message is relevant and worth listening to. In addition, you must be totally sold on your ideas and use enthusiasm to pull people into your positive energy and direction.

On a similar note, it's almost embarrassing to put this next piece of advice in the book, but it's worth noting. People DO judge you on your looks and appearance. Get over it. We all do it. If this is true, then why do so many people look like slobs? I'm not joking. Think of how many bad tattoos or body piercings you've seen in everyday life? Yes, if you decide to tattoo a past romance on your neck or wrists, people will notice them. I meet far too many people at all levels in business that've missed or chosen to ignore the memo about dressing for success. Their casual look is costing them not only influence, business, but also in today's tight job market, a first or second interview. If you're going to play the part, you need to look the part. Enough said.

**#4. Have a great commercial.** As we discussed earlier in this chapter, you must create and use a powerful elevator or 15-second commercial in all your interactions. This is non-negotiable in my book, as opportunities are around us each and every day that most people either miss or do poorly. Use the power of first impressions to your advantage to engage and attract opportunities into your world.

**#5. Get in their mind.** I work with a lot of people to help them solve and get better at the marketing and sales processes within their organizations. Two common complaints I hear involve finding ways to generate repeat business and handle customers who leave them over the issue of price. When I sit down with many of these people, a very revealing and disturbing pattern often emerges. They know little if anything about their customers. There's no relationship. It's a façade. They haven't taken the time to discover, listen closely (see point #2 again) and note what makes their best customers tick.

Instead of being a valued business partner, many of them are vendors in the mind of their customer. Mere order takers who've taken their livelihood and others' business for granted. It's a common illness during good economic times that becomes painfully obvious when things tighten up and aggressive competitors go on the attack. Yes, knowing about your customers' dreams, goals, hobbies and family is valuable to not just the bottom line, but also to build a stronger relationship.

**#6. Share success stories.** Weave into all your communications good news from your best sales people: satisfied customers. Share with others the impact and value from your customers' point of view not just your own. I'm amazed at how many people still use corporate speak and complex terms to describe what they do. They recite and brag about the company, product or service and the prospect either tunes them out or becomes bored to tears.

The more specific you are with your success stories the better the impact. For example, if you work with law firms as a key client group, share a recent success story with another prospective law firm at your next meeting. Of course, do this only if you're granted expressed written permission to do so and it doesn't breach client confidentiality or terms of your existing agreement. Alright, enough disclaimers!

**#7. Be brief.** In the age of information overload and massive distraction, when you capture someone, you must work quickly. The days of marathon meetings are ending, especially in most corporate America circles. Firms are doing more with less, and the ability to get to the point and engage people in a memorable way are the keys to persuasive communication. Tighten up your presentations, phone calls, proposals, electronic messages and lead with your best ideas and benefits. Speed is your ally.

For example, why are the most effective videos on YouTube one to three minutes in length? Simple: They get watched, require little time commitment and are easy to digest and spread around.

Here are two simple and powerful equations to burn into your mind regarding decision makers that I've learned from years of experience that will save you time and help you determine who's really involved in the buying process:

**True Decision makers = shorter meetings**
**Non-decision makers = longer meetings**

As a special thank you for investing in this book we have several free audios for you to gain additional insights from other world-class thought leaders mentioned in this book. Go to www.MindCaptureBook.com/bonus.php to access several free downloads including my one-on-one interview with world-class networking guru Dr. Ivan Misner, founder of Business Network International (BNI). Enjoy and remember, as he'd say: *Givers Gain™*.

Now, let's move into chapter nine and explore why you must work on building authenticity into all of your communications and several smart ways to do so.

## CHAPTER 9

# Building Authenticity in a Cynical Digital World

*"The ability to create demand for any product or service increases substantially once positive word-of-mouth and credibility have been established in the digital realm."*
-Tony Rubleski

THE GAME'S ALMOST UP. There are few places left to hide. In the age of instant search, you and your organization's reputation are now only a keystroke away for the world to discover. Transparency online is becoming the new norm. This is one of the positive consequences of the digital age. In paradox, a new scam is launched online each day while simultaneously another is found out and put out of business. Subsequently, managing and building a solid online reputation are the newest tools and skills to add to your marketing arsenal.

Here's a quick reminder from the second *Mind Capture* book to set the stage for this chapter: We all have a built in BS Meter when it comes to marketing messages of any kind. Let's take a closer look at what I call "persuasion nets" in our minds that often build up over time with cynicism and doubt when we're confronted with most marketing messages. Here are a few key persuasion nets that shape our BS Meter in relation to marketing messages:

**Managing Overload:** The typical North American is hit with an average of 3000+ marketing messages per day, and the number keeps increasing.

**Societal Programming:** Sales is a "dirty word" to most people even though everyone is engaged in selling, whether they realize it or not.

**Time Challenges:** In a sped up digital world, we're all trying to maximize and manage time.

**The Choice Paradox:** We love having options, but it often stifles our ability to discern and in many situations make a decision.

**Short Attention Spans:** This is only going to intensify in a real-time mobile talk, text and online-driven world.

**Sales Baggage:** This is often not discussed by many marketing pros, but it is very real. It's the past experiences, good and bad, related to sales that impact and shape how we trust or distrust any marketing message when it appears or "captures" us on our mental radar.

**Age:** Time is a great teacher and the more life experience we accumulate, the higher degree of habit force and pattern recognition that occurs when we sense or pick up on messaging that attempts to persuade or sell us.

## Why You Must Work On Building Authenticity Each Day for Yourself & Your Organization

Knowing how challenging it is these days to get what I call "Mind Capture" with people, it's essential that you lead with your strongest marketing bullets or evidence when engaging prospects directly or indirectly in the offline or online space. To keep and engage people, you must quickly demonstrate why they might have a need for what you do, but more importantly, why they should possibly believe that your claims are real.

In the age of instant search and massive choice, your ability to lower the BS Meter with skeptical prospects isn't easy. However, as we'll soon discuss, there are several timeless and new strategies that when combined will help you build evidence in your own marketing efforts to quickly differentiate, and persuade with maximum effectiveness.

With a tightening economy, here's another major reason authenticity is so important: The competition will often make attempts to discredit you, undercut prices, and make false claims out of pure desperation. A great reputation and strong marketing evidence in your arsenal helps to not only diffuse the competition, but also attract powerful referrals via word-of-mouth in both the physical world and the "word-of-mouse" online world.

### Seven Powerful Ways to Help You Build Authenticity Both Online and Offline in a Cynical Digital World

1. Collect and use customer testimonials
2. Create and share relevant content of interest
3. Give value first and your sales pitch second
4. Become active within the community via cause marketing
5. Leverage all positive press related to you and your industry (reprints of print articles, links to radio/TV or online features)
6. Use the personal touch and customize ALL communications if possible
7. Associate and partner with other well-known people and companies

**#1. Collect and use customer testimonials.** What someone else says about you is a thousand times more believable than what you say about yourself. Burn that last sentence into your mind and never forget it. This is a timeless strategy that is becoming even more important in today's sped up, crowded and confusing market place. In the age of instant online search, your authenticity is on the line for the entire world to see, and it must be easy for a skeptical prospect to find. Here are a few tips to help you get more testimonials:

- Earn them
- Ask for them
- Capture them quickly
- Make it easy to receive them
- If possible, get them on video
- Always tell the person you ask the reason for your request
- Make sure you get permission from the other person to share his or her comments with others

Right now the best testimonials are those captured on video. A short one to two-minute video testimonial from a key customer can do wonders to build authenticity and save valuable time in your marketing process.

**#2. Create and share relevant content of interest.** In the age of information overload, it is essential that you think of yourself as a media channel that offers relevant content to those who are in the process of discovering, considering or are currently working with you. As Chris Anderson brilliantly sums up in his book, *The Long Tail*, we are a nation of niches. In a niche world, people expect specific information related to what you can do to help or serve them. The more specific you are with targeted information such as articles, links, white papers, blogs, books, video, etc., the more you are positioned and perceived as the authentic thought leader and best choice within your industry.

A quick online search can uncover a treasure trove of articles and links that you can share and use to expand your influence with others. In addition, key vendors and referral partners often have lots of great content and updates available for you to use. Here's a quick and handy checklist of content options available to guide and inspire you that we covered in the second *Mind Capture* book:

- Newsletter
- Webinars
- Facebook comments
- Eletter
- YouTube
- Podcasts
- Blogs
- Seminars
- Press releases
- Special events
- Articles
- Reviews
- Recorded message/hotline
- Voice broadcasting
- Special reports
- Teleconferences
- Twitter updates
- Case studies
- MySpace
- White papers
- Video links
- Video demonstrations
- Panels and forums
- Survey results
- Books
- Product launches, or updates
- Fax updates or bulletins
- Local/regional radio show, TV segment, or column

**#3. Give value first and your sales pitch second.** The age of the heavy-handed sales pitch is drawing to a close. In a transparent, online world loaded with options, intense competition, and smarter customers, a new age of selling is dawning. However, most people are still missing the boat. I base a lot of this opinion on the huge number of websites I see that add little value or differentiation to their target audience. Many people continue to ignore and resist this major paradigm shift taking place before their eyes and keyboards.

As we discussed in point number two, one of the smartest ways to add value and separate yourself from the pack is via educating and sharing great content with others. In addition to providing content, offering a reward, promotion or bonus for spending time with you and your message is a smart and timeless lead-generation strategy. You make the reward or offer after first proving that you are relevant and have added value to the person's life.

This is a challenge for most people to grasp and requires a switch in thinking from being secretive to being open and willing to share. In the age of two-way digital communication and instant online search, people look for and seek out people and firms that are upfront and make their ability easily known that they can solve problems quickly and easily. Yes, your competition may check you out, but so what? If you're that afraid to share information with no guarantees of a prospect choosing to do business with you, then maybe you're in the wrong business. The new age of digital authenticity will require growth in your faith and capacity to share and educate prospects along the various points of the buying cycle. This is another enlightening contribution to capitalism that will be required for the long-term growth and word-of-mouth potential of successful organizations today and into the future.

**#4. Become active within the community via cause marketing.** In the second *Mind Capture* book, I describe in chapter seven, *The Cause*, why partnering with a local, regional or international non-profit you truly are passionate about is not just a great way to give back, but also a way to build goodwill and credibility for you and your company.

In addition, many non-profits are a great vehicle to partner with and get your message out by sponsoring or donating your products and services to raise funds and help out. If the non-profit does mailings, media or fundraising events to current donors and partners you pick up positive exposure and also become known within their community at the same time.

Again, let me clearly state that I believe you should give or get involved with non-profits that you're truly passionate about, with the intent to help first and get your name out second. Good PR, visibility and meeting sharp people are of course possible benefits, but they should not be the primary objective.

**#5. Leverage all positive press related to you and your industry.** If you or your company receives positive press for your efforts, make sure to leverage this and share it with key clients, referral partners, and prospects within your various communications channels. The media are very influential, so use this positive goodwill to remind others that your business is adding value to the marketplace and active in the community or industry. We instinctively will believe a media article or interview versus the best paid advertisement. Again, what someone else says about us is much more credible and believable in the eyes of a prospect.

People are attracted to successful people that they know, like and trust. Far too many businesses downplay the impact that a positive article or review pertaining to their company, employees or customers has on others. In addition, in an age of fragmented media and short media cycles, the odds are also high that most people may not have seen the article, review or heard a radio, TV or web-based media interview when it first appeared. Repurpose and use this third-party media proof over and over again within your marketing efforts. This again helps to make the case that your company is legit and has a unique story that is clearly different from the competition.

**#6. Use the personal touch whenever possible.** Good old fashioned manners such as "please" and "thank you" can do wonders. Such things as sending a hand-written note or thank you card, gift or telephone call go a long, long way in the age of digital. It's not uncommon that I'll get a thank you email or call back from someone who's received a genuine thank you voicemail message from me. Simple on the surface, yet so few people do it. We use and recommend a stay in touch system called SendOutCards. If you'd like more information, please send me an email directly (Tony@MindCaptureGroup. com) with the Subject Line: Information on SOC. A person on our team will follow up with details.

I'm amazed at how many people that I do business with never acknowledge or thank me for my business and referrals. The highest compliment any business can receive is a referral.

**#7. Associate and partner with other well-known people and companies in your area or industry.** Borrowing others' goodwill, reputation, feedback and experience is a smart way to quickly build authenticity. In today's current economic climate, people are carefully evaluating who they spend their time and money with during the sales process. We make lots of snap decisions each day and we often choose well-known firms because they deliver a consistent product or service time and time again based on their reputation and sustained track record of success.

For example, let's take a page from the book business. It's well known in the publishing business that positive advance reviews from other well-known and successful authors is key for new and up and coming authors to help gain potential book buyers' and reviewers' fleeting time and attention. The amount of new books released each day is staggering, and with limited bookstore space available, the competition is fierce. Leveraging other successful author and media endorsements is of high importance for every author and publisher in the quest to promote their work and stand out from the pack.

Now that we've covered seven powerful strategies to connect and build authenticity online and offline in a cynical digital world, let's turn our attention to the awesome power that capturing our dreams and goals into written form plays in the awakening process.

## CHAPTER 10:

# The Power of Lists

*"How often do we see new opportunities come our way,*
*get excited about those opportunities, but find ourselves*
*unable to take advantage because we have some old,*
*limiting belief that we are still hanging onto?"*
-Kody Bateman

IT CHALLENGES ME WHEN I FIND myself thinking about or seeing people conspiring each day against their own greatness because their inner thoughts are out of purposeful alignment. In addition to this problem, "misery loves company" type of thinking and behavior is now celebrated, packaged and sold on hundreds of daily talk shows and TV programs up and down the dial. Millions of people are addicted to and negatively influenced by it.

The ratings and market for negative-based media and information speaks volumes about our society and the priorities, or shall I say lack of priorities, that people give to their time, talents and abilities to positively serve others. While a few people who read the last sentence may feel that this is arrogant or mean spirited, that's fine with me. If it offends someone and wakes them up to take a better look at their own life to improve it, versus simply complaining and watching others' lives, then I'm on track with this book.

It's amazing these days how we have millions of people who claim they can't find more "time" to learn a new skill, find a better job or start a part-time business, but still spend multiple hours each day in front of their computers or flat screen TVs frittering away their skills and potential greatness. With modern technology, creature comforts and unlimited amounts of competing options for free time now available, it will become more of a challenge to resist distraction, unless you deliberately change and grow your thinking, habits, associations and beliefs about success and achievement. If you require more clarity, go back and reread the section in chapter three related to the power of habit force and the benefits of having a champion mindset versus a disempowering one.

For example, it's amazing to me how many people obsessively watch other people's lives through reality-based TV shows. Now, full disclosure, I watch a show or two myself, but I'm more concerned with those who watch several hours each day and then complain how bad their own life is based on what they see. Most of these shows are seductive, interesting, entertaining and cleverly scripted and edited to weave the illusion of being 100% real.

Many loyal viewers use these shows as an escape and never realize that they're taking their own valuable life force and meddling into other people's drama, instead of creating and living their own dream. If this describes you, then I'll tell you up front to please snap out of this mental trap and illusion. This chapter will be like a healthy dose of smelling salts to wake up your mind to not just a different way of viewing the world, but positively acting upon it. Here's a bold proclamation to set the tone of where we'll journey over the next few pages:

**It's time to shut off the negative shows in your head, computer and TV screen, and start scripting your own life for excellence and achievement.**

We have too many people watching and waiting, when they should be focused on investing more time designing and carrying out their own plan! To help set the stage for scripting your own life for the better, we'll explore several forms of lists that are essential to create, review and take action upon **each day** that will serve you well.

### The Bucket List

In this wonderful movie starring Morgan Freeman and Jack Nicholson, the two main characters discover they both don't have much time left to live. In response to the diagnosis, they become inspired to create a list of powerful goals or a "Bucket List" of things to accomplish together before they both die.

So here's my challenge and exercise for you to really think about. What if you were told you only had six months left to live? After the shock wears off, what do you do next? Stay with me here; this is a big mind bender I'm going to share with you. If you've read this far, I thank you, and know that you're ready for the place I'm going to now take you.

**The Goal Isn't To Bring You Down, But To Get You To Rise Up and Reclaim Your Inner Genius NOW and Without Further Delay!**

I've seen many people in my own life, including my own father; turn the initial death sentence of six months or a year left to live, into a **live life to the fullest sentence**. I'll explain. They treated these remaining days like gold, without inhibition and the key phrase: without fear! What if we all lived this way? What a very different world it would be. I sense that many people would treat each day with a passion and intensity that would marvel and inspire themselves and those around them.

Father time is strange indeed. When we're children life moves at a crawl, and when we're adults it begins to pick up speed like a snowball rolling downhill. We cannot go back in time and rewrite or live in the past. Nor should we allow the two thieves known as regret and guilt to haunt and steal our valuable time known as the present. An untrained, negative, and beaten down mind filled with regret and fear is much more dangerous to success than most people realize or can even imagine.

## The Honor List

The names and dates are unfamiliar to most people, but to me they are pivotal markers and turning points in my destiny and journey.

| | | |
|---|---|---|
| Stan Rubleski | 1984 | Age: 46 |
| Robert Austin | 1985 | Age: 19 |
| Dan Hutchinson | 1993 | Age: 21 |
| Craig Shriver | 1995 | Age: 22 |

Four names, four years in time, four major people who left an impression on my soul and present state of how I look at motivation and action. Like a bright, burning, orange flare in a pitch black forest, each one of them grabbed my soul and uniquely changed my destiny in ways that no one could imagine or possibly link together.

## Frozen In Time, But Never Forgotten

The years and ages of Stan, Robert, Dan and Craig represent the year they exited the game of physical life. Their life clocks here on Earth ran out of time quickly and far too soon. Two of them passed from cancer and two of them were involved in freak accidents.

While many people these days obsessively worry about retirement and multiple "what-if" scenarios as to what they'll be doing when they turn 50, 60 or 70 years of age, this was not an option for the four people I've listed. Unfortunately, they never had the chance to fill their minds with such trivia, for their life force was snuffed out at relatively young ages. It's ok and healthy to dream and think of the future, but sadly, most people obsess and worry relentlessly about a future date or marker in time that may burn out before they even get there. Each day thousands of people are notified that their life will end soon, while others get no warning at all.

### The List of Four Exercise

I'm a big believer in creating and using lists to get things done quicker and with less stress. Yes, for men it's wired into our DNA. This next exercise is designed to make you appreciate the life and talents you might be taking for granted at this moment in time. I'm going to have you create a very different type of list that you may have never thought about making and move it from your head into the physical realm via pen and paper. Be prepared, this will also conjure up many strong emotions from your past.

If we sat down over a cup of coffee and I said to you, *"Write your own list of four people who've passed on and how they positively impacted your life."* Which names and reasons would you put on the list and why?

I want you to do this right now. Take a few minutes and write their names on a piece of paper or in the spaces provided here.

1. _____
2. _____
3. _____
4. _____

The ages and dates of the names on my own list of four serve as a stiff reminder to me that death is a part of our existence and can come in the prime of life with some advance warning and often when we least expect it. The goal here of creating your own list of names is to remind you to deeply think about your own life, appreciate it, and look at each day as a gift to be celebrated and lived fully even during the hourly ups and downs. If you made up *The List of Four* for yourself, welcome to the club. I now urge you to honor these people in your life by going after your dreams and passions with a renewed sense of urgency.

A second question: *Is your current life honoring them or would they wonder why you're squandering it?* This isn't an easy question to ask, yet alone think about. However, it's essential for you to dig deep within your own life story and answer this question. Again, the goal is to allow these people who were in your life to inspire you to rise up and cultivate your inner genius.

Look, every human who's ever lived, past or present, has made trade-offs. I believe true life balance is one of the biggest myths still being packaged and sold across the radio and TV talk show circuit to society. It's sexy to talk about "work and life balance," but achieving it is not easy. Many times when we're in flow or actively pursuing a big goal, creative chaos will take over and mess with balance. It will happen, trust me. It's important to continually gain perspective and work towards recognizing that a short-term imbalance is often required to help us in the long term to see our dreams take shape.

Finally, let me ask you a third question that few people, especially those in business, rarely if ever stop and slow down to ask themselves: *What really drives and inspires you to play the game?* Each of us gives up most of our waking hours and valuable life force to work for someone else or to build and pursue our own enterprise. There are no timeouts in life, so let me ask you once again, *what **really** drives you to play the game?* In the sped up, digital, interruption based, media overload society, many people are getting bogged down in distraction and worry about what others are doing, thinking, saying, writing or watching instead of focusing on themselves.

If you aren't motivated, focused and truly sold on your dreams for the life you're living and designing for significance, then how in the world will you pull it off and attract the people and resources needed to carry it out? When these ingredients are missing, a mental tug-of-war takes place and sabotages many good-intentioned people.

I wrote this entire book, along with the exercises it contains, to be more than just a book that you simply read and put back on the shelf. I want it to also serve as an action guide for you to discover new lessons so you can learn to cultivate and grow your inner genius. You and I are travelers on the journey called life. We may have never met, but I can tell you one key thing we both share: We want more from life. We often see the positive potential in others and we're curious to discover ways to keep growing.

**Three Other <u>Essential</u> Lists To Serve You Well As You
Reinvent and Reclaim Your Inner Genius**

1. **Gratitude list**
2. **Goodbye list**
3. **Goals list**

**Gratitude list.** In my written journal, I have a list of 78 things I'm grateful for each day. It's in the front of my journal next to my goals and covers a wide range of items including God, family, health, friends, travel, music, past accomplishments, and on and on. When you create your own gratitude list and review it each day or pull it out when you're having a challenging day, you'll be amazed at how it will change your mindset for the better.

*"Reflect upon your present blessings, of which everyone has many; not
on your past misfortunes of which all people have some."*
-Charles Dickens

**Goodbye list.** Very few people do the next written exercise that I'm about to describe. I urge you to do it immediately. It will seem unconventional and strange at first, but please stay with me and resist reading past this as it's essential in helping you remove negative past associations, anger and guilt within your own unique life story.

In the spaces below, I ask that you take a minute or two to write down the name(s) of those who have caused grief, stress or undue mental anguish in your past that you need to forgive and remove from your mental space. To jog your mental archives, here are the most common areas to draw from: family, career, school, religion, friends and acquaintances.

Name(s):

_____  _____  _____  _____

_____  _____  _____  _____

_____  _____  _____  _____

Now, I need you to quickly grab a piece of blank paper nearby. Take the names you've just listed and write them on the sheet of paper. Now, take the freshly written page of names, review the list carefully, and say out loud:

*I forgive each of you; it's time to move on with my life. Goodbye.*

After you've done this, pick up the paper and slowly crinkle it into a ball and throw it away.

**Here are several reasons this is such a powerful mental exercise:**

- You free up your mind by letting go of old negative emotions such as guilt, anger and fear associated with these people.

- It helps you to create greater clarity and focus in pursuing the new, empowering goals and outcomes you seek within your life.

- When you forgive others, which is not easy for most of us to do, you'll realize that we all are flawed human beings, and the negative emotions we once held not only wasted our precious time, but blocked our ability to achieve and attract better people and outcomes into our lives.

- By writing these names down, speaking out loud the statement I just described above and physically taking action by rolling the paper into a ball and throwing it away, we anchor into our minds the seriousness of our intentions.

**Goals list**. Yes, the foundation to your mental house is important and having your goals written down and reviewed often is non-negotiable. Many of you reading this book already know this, but many people still skip this step or are hearing this advice for the very first time. I suggest that you create a 'Top

10' one-year goal list and also a list of life-time goals, similar to the bucket list, which you check off over the course of your life to inspire and fire you up. In addition, this will intensify the joy you receive when you look at your gratitude list.

Another powerful personal development strategy that ties in with setting goals is to create a detailed written list of "I am" statements. Here's a quick explanation. Take the key items from the various lists we just created and write them down as positive, present tense affirmations you read, review and recite daily as part of your new success habits.

Here are a few of my own "I am" statements to share and help you get started in creating your own list:

*I am grateful to God for each day of life and his blessings*
*I am a wonderful father and parent*
*I am healthy in body, mind and spirit*
*I am positively influencing millions of people with my passion and gifts*
*I am in awe each day and pay-it-forward*
*I am honoring each day my Lord, my family and my list of four*
*I am one of the top professional speakers in the world*
*I am enjoying laughter, music and beauty each day*
*I am taking many trips per year with my family*

In his wonderful book titled, *Promptings*, author Kody Bateman explains in-depth the positive power this mental exercise has when applied properly to your own life. In our own minds, we make statements and judgments about ourselves and others thousands of times each day. Unfortunately, most of it is negative and defeating unless we deliberately set out to override the old programming with positive mental software as we've explored throughout this book.

The law of attraction was given a big boost in 2006 with Rhonda Byrne's bestselling book and film, *The Secret*. While many gained a whole new perspective, others downplayed it and often mocked its intent and powerful message. Regardless of the critics, the law of attraction isn't a joke or strange mental voodoo. It's quite real and if you're tuned in and turned on each day mentally, you'll see it in action within your own life and those around you.

I commend you for taking action on the items we shared in this chapter, for they set up a wonderful bridge to where we'll go in the next chapter. Let's examine why the ability to customize and connect with others in your life are valuable skills to master in your ongoing quest to achieve and share your genius and gifts with the world.

## CHAPTER 11:
# Customize to Connect

*"In the age of digital communication, high touch personalized communication still works best!"*
-Tony Rubleski

MASS ADVERTISING AND MESSAGING are losing both credibility and effectiveness for a variety of reasons. I described these in chapter nine as persuasion nets that shape our own BS Meter in relation to marketing messages. **Here are six additional reasons it's of key importance to customize your communications to help you get Mind Capture with your marketing messages:**

1.  The ability to niche market messages is becoming much easier to pull off.

2.  The customer of today is becoming more and more resistant to mass messaging due to time shifting and new tools created specifically to filter out ads – think TIVO, podcasts, YouTube, etc.

3.  People are burned out and even offended by marketers that are woefully still trying to cram a square message into a round hole.

4.  In the age of free content, information, and a sea of competing choices, people's expectations and appetite for customized solutions are quickly becoming the norm.

5.  If you don't differentiate and add value – perceived or real – then you risk losing profit margins and move into the realm of becoming a commodity in your marketplace.

6.  In a tightening economy, people are more price sensitive, pickier, and often wait longer to make decisions in the selection process.

Marketing legend Dan Kennedy describes the marketing process with the following simple, yet brilliant statement:

> *"Marketing is getting the right message to the right people via the right media and methods."*

Let me narrow your search and share with you ten smart ways to customize and make your communications memorable. Top marketers use these techniques to build Mind Capture with people in an ever increasingly noisy and saturated media universe. Some you've heard me mention earlier in the book, while others are being presented for the first time. They are based on my own 20+ years of studying and applying marketing and persuasion strategies in a wide range of industries with thousands of people.

## 10 POWERFUL TIPS FOR CUSTOMIZING YOUR MESSAGE TO CAPTURE OTHERS

1.  **Use the person's name in your message(s).** The most important word in any person's mind is his or her own name. Mass marketing is dying; customization is the new norm. If you do any form of direct mail or email

marketing, this is a huge way to bump up readability. From the outside envelope, to the headline of your letter or email subject line, to the salutation, the recipient's name should be included for maximum results.

2. **Use custom mailings such as cards, articles, or an unexpected gift or thank you note.** I love direct mail. While more and more companies are foolishly abandoning it for a variety of reasons which I will not waste space arguing here, all I can say is that many smart businesses and non-profits use it with outstanding results. Take away all my marketing tools if you must, but leave me with a pen, card and a postage stamp and I can connect with almost anyone.

3. **Employ humor and make people laugh. Business is far too stuffy and "corporate" these days.** Always remember that real people, not focus groups or company yes men, are the folks you're trying to reach. An often overlooked way to capture people is to get them laughing. It's a positive emotion you should employ in your communications. I'm not going to tell you how and when to use it. You know your customers better than anyone else. Tune into them, do what's comfortable, and get them laughing. Positive reaction, word-of-mouth and new sales are often the byproducts of this strategy.

4. **Reveal something unique about yourself.** As a professional speaker, I have the honor to get in front of thousands of people each year. Without a doubt, what helps me build a bridge with my audiences is the use of stories from my own life. I reveal memorable moments that often center around our pets and family. I enjoy telling the stories and the lessons learned. Based on comments I get from the audiences and meeting planners, they appreciate me sharing other shades of what makes me tick versus strictly business.

Here are a few ideas and areas of interest to get the ball rolling:

- Fun or memorable stories related to family, friends and customers
- An award or accomplishment you or a key business associate have earned
- Your successes and failures and the lessons learned from each
- Hobbies or things you enjoy doing outside of work
- Causes you believe in and give time, energy or monetary resources

5. **Offer free content or tips that improve lives or situations.** This is a must these days. As we've mentioned several times throughout this book, the customer is buried with choice which often creates confusion and hesitation in the influence process. Your mission is to bring them to the conclusion that you are the superior choice and worthy of their business. One of the smartest ways to do this is via the use of great content, online and offline, to educate and differentiate yourself from the competition.

   Let me say it again: The age of the heavy handed sales pitch is almost done. It's two minutes to midnight and the time is now to make your move and add this strategy into your online and offline communications.

6. **Be brief and promise speed.** Think YouTube and Twitter for a second. Short, direct and engaging is the new norm. People are buried in information and lack the necessary filters and time to sort through it all. An interesting way to combat this huge problem we all face is to clearly telegraph in your communications a promise of speed. As noted earlier in the book, when seeking a phone or face-to-face appointment with a prospect, it's to your benefit to promise that you won't take up much time. Honor this, and if things are going well you can always ask permission for more time or a second meeting. Let the other person know you're busy too so they get a sense that even if what you propose isn't a fit, you won't lead them into a trap of wasting their valuable time.

7. **Send a short video message or greeting.** I can tell you that in the last few months this is one of my favorite ways to blast through message clutter and capture people. I argue that a custom video message sent by you not only will get viewed almost every time, but more importantly it will leave the recipient "wowed" because it's so different than what everyone else is doing.

   Capturing and sharing video has gotten ridiculously easy. For example, I use a combination of professional video for certain marketing initiatives and FlipVideo® for real-time video such as sending greetings or capturing happy customer testimonials.

8. **Make a thank you phone call.** Yes, pick up the good old phone and reach out and touch someone. Does that last sentence sound familiar? In the age of texting, tweeting, poking, and sharing comments, the telephone is still a powerful way to cut through and connect with anyone. In the age of social media, many people skip this strategy and downplay its importance. I caution you to resist the temptation and allure to just send digital communications only. If you employ a **balance** of communications with customers, referral partners and prospects, your ability to influence and connect with more people will greatly increase.

   Granted, it's harder to get people on the phone these days, you can still work wonders by leaving a short, crisp thank you message. It used to be the primary way people communicated and it's becoming a novelty as people are going more and more digital. The biggest argument I get with this strategy is that people don't have the time to make a phone call. Come on, are you kidding me? Excuse me here for just a few seconds. If it's one of your key customers or contacts, I certainly hope you come down from your ivory tower Mr. or Mrs. I'm Too Important, and pick up the good old phone. If not, your competition will.

Use the trend of digital laziness and distraction to your marketing advantage to help you stand out from the herd.

9.  **Share stories.** Here's timeless sales advice worth sharing that I heard years ago at a seminar: Facts tell, stories sell. Timeless wisdom that far too many sales reps, marketing directors and even high-level corporate executives still ignore and foolishly downplay. So why do most people still not use the power of storytelling? I'll push a few buttons right now and offer up my best answer. Most people have no clear plan of persuasion and often forget to make the use of success stories a staple in their communications.

    The best storytellers cast a spell on people and pull them into an almost magnetic trance. Once they've cast the spell, it's hard not to engage them and add several levels of credibility to their claims, especially if it's a story that directly relates to the customer or prospect's life or current situation.

10. **Ask powerful questions to get people thinking.** Oh, the power of a great question. If asked at the right time, it can freeze someone and get them thinking in a whole new light.  I'm often asked by others why I ask so many questions. I quickly respond that my rationale is simple and strategic in nature: Questions engage the mind. You should have a list of what I call "mind benders" at your disposal within all of your communications. These questions are designed to make a customer or prospect think of you as someone who "gets it" and understands them at a much different and deeper level than others.

Now that we've shared several powerful ways to connect with and engage others, let's head into the home stretch. We'll look at why becoming and staying a student of life is essential to your ongoing success and ability to continually grow your inner entrepreneurial genius.

## CHAPTER 12:

# A Student of Life

*"If you are going to do anything, you must expect criticism. But it's better to be a doer than a critic. The doer moves; the critic stands still, and is passed by."*

-Bruce Barton

### The World Needs You To Stop Worrying, Step Up Your Game and Truly Start Living

EACH OF US HAS A COMPLEX, wonderful mind that either serves us or enslaves us. As we've discovered within these pages, the decision on how we use it is purely up to each of us. As we head into the last section of this book, here's a quick reminder list of five key areas that influence our minds and whether we achieve the life we truly desire or a life of frustration, regret and disappointment. When you assess each of these areas, you should be able to determine whether they're helping you grow your entrepreneurial genius or if they're holding you back.

1.  **HABIT FORCE**
2.  **ATTITUDE**
3.  **WITH WHOM WE ASSOCIATE**
4.  **KNOWLEDGE**
5.  **QUESTIONS WE ASK**

In several chapters, we discussed why it's critical to take back your mind and several ways to do it. No more waiting. No sugar-coating allowed. Excuse time is over. The world is ready. We need you to step up, discover and promote your talents, passion and solution-based ideas to help yourself and others in a world mired in negative thinking, resentments and constant fear.

Advice is everywhere you turn these days. Most of it is sadly misguided and designed to suppress and curb people's unique talents and ideas. Despite what others say, good or bad, if you're still not 100% sold on your own inner genius **each day**, the risk is high that you'll get distracted and drift away from pursuing your genius when the many forces such as negative people and other "fear peddlers" attempt to sabotage and knock you off course. You must reprogram, cultivate, and defend your mind and dreams daily.

### Was This A Self-Help Book or A Business Book?

My intent was to design this book to be a combination of both. I firmly believe that solid personal development skills and continual expansion of your business knowledge are much more intertwined and of even greater importance during this time of great economic change. The best analogy is to imagine yourself trying to start up a lawn mower without first checking the gas tank to see if it has any gas. When you have to pull the cord several more times than usual to get the lawn mower started, you'll often get more and more frustrated because you're unaware of the fact that the lawn mower is out of fuel. You have the machine, but no fuel to get it started to complete the job at hand.

Sadly, the lawn mower example just described is how far too many people are living today. They're aware and sense problems within their own life and feel an inner restlessness. This unease keeps building because they often never slow down long enough to reexamine the course of events within their life and ways to change the present situation for the better. They get frustrated, give up or end up quitting way too soon because their mind, similar to the lawn mower fuel tank, is empty and needs fuel to run properly. Seeking positive mental fuel for your mind is required in a world intoxicated with fear-based messaging and massive distraction tempting us to lose sight of what really matters in our lives.

The classic poet Ralph Waldo Emerson summed it up best when he wrote that most people lead lives of quiet desperation. What a shame and tragedy that this happens in an age of massive possibility and countless opportunity. A huge abundance of knowledge and collective wisdom from super successful people is now readily available today at little or no cost. This level of shared genius that most people take for granted or dismiss would boggle the minds of people from past generations if they were still alive to see how things have changed.

Most people believe and never question the "traditional" educational structures of studying primarily facts and logic and scoff at the massive power of personal development. How tragic that they allow unhappy people and often fear-based misinformation to make a mockery of this powerful knowledge. There are always two sides to every story. By design, I put the "fear peddlers" on trial in the beginning of this book, so you can judge and decide for yourself if you want to keep buying and believing what they're selling. Yes, you do have choices and options available if you open your mind, do your homework, ask empowering questions and rediscover your own unique genius.

Yes, the book focuses heavily on why it's important to work on your own skill sets and on **improving your mind every day.** Here's why it must become a new ingrained habit: there's a risk when reading business books or attending seminars (I speak from experience) that you'll get fired up for a few hours or a few days, try a couple of new things you've learned, see a little burst of positive change and then fall right back into old unproductive habits and limiting beliefs. Our own ego, combined with a toxic mix of negative people and societal programming, will work extremely hard to sabotage new behaviors and beliefs when feeling uncomfortable and threatened. The biggest battle we all face is a negative and undisciplined mind!

I congratulate you for taking the trip with me to awaken your entrepreneurial genius and making it to the last few pages of this book. You have gone further than most people would or usually do when they pick up a book with strong intentions but often a weak ability to achieve reading it completely. I'm honored to have shared valuable time, lessons, and wisdom from others and my own unfolding life journey within these pages.

However, the journey isn't over; it's a continual work in progress. For some of you, this new journey and way of thinking and living may be very new and exhilarating. For the experienced veterans of personal development, it is my sincere wish that the book has helped to reaffirm and push you to stay the course with tenacity and a renewed sense of optimism. It will be required even more during this time of great economic change and massive amounts of negative influence attempting to distract and plant seeds of doubt and fear.

### Your Final Mission, Should You Choose To Accept It

Let me leave you with three tips related to your own life journey going forward to keep you inspired and your powerful inner genius burning bright.

1. **Learn something new each day.** The activities and list exercises you completed in this book should be reviewed each day to remind you of key areas of importance to focus on as you awaken and build your entrepreneurial genius. I strongly recommend getting and keeping an updated written journal that you carry with you at all times. This provides you the ability to capture, create and reflect upon the ideas and goals you seek to put in play

and strive toward. For maximum learning and retention, I recommend you transfer over your notes from this book to your personal success journal to easyily access, review, monitor and add new items of interest.

Also, I strongly encourage you to explore the resources and thought leaders presented in the *Additional FREE Resources* and *Additional Books to Engage & Awaken Your Mind* sections that follow. You have an exciting journey ahead of you and there are many other wise teachers and knowledge to draw upon for inspiration, insights and assistance.

2. **Look for the life lesson in each success or temporary setback you experience.** Self-reflection is a powerful talent and blessing from God to be utilized for wisdom, improvement and good. In a sped up digital world, slowing down and disconnecting at the end of the day or on the weekend to analyze and reflect upon the week is incredibly good to do. A major clue to why people experience either success or failure on a consistent basis in their own life is built upon how they view, monitor and reflect upon the lessons learned from the unique experiences of each day.

We must never forget in the midst of life's complexities, ebbs and flows, that we all have a choice each day when we awaken: We can grow, adapt and keep learning from a combination of the past (wisdom) and present moment (improvement), or we can choose the path of apathy and a negative mindset to stifle our growth, talents and abilities to see the potential beauty and learning lessons that life brings us each day. Again, capturing the distinctions and lessons from our daily lives and writing them down is another reason that keeping a life journal is so incredibly valuable.

3. **Strive to pass on your wisdom, legacy and genius to others.** If someone would have told me 17 years ago, at the age of 20 and in college, that I'd be reading, learning, and writing at an even faster progression in my

thirties, I would have thought they were joking. Yes, time does give us the blessing of perspective, yet I mention my own learning experience and evolution from the factory floor to the board room for one key reason: You have unique wisdom, talents, stories and genius that can and should be shared with others. However, you must have the courage and passion to share it with others despite the naysayers. There will never be another you. You are one-of-a-kind. Everything you've experienced is a lesson in disguise whether you know it or not. Take a deep breath, smile and realize that you're a miracle. Let no one else attempt to sabotage or fool you into thinking otherwise.

I'm often intrigued by how many people I know that work towards the societal goal of "retirement" and quickly discover that it's often not what they thought it would or should be. After a life of productive activity and being in the game, many agents of change and successful entrepreneurs go bonkers after a few months of travel, sleep and golf. To turn off their talents and inner genius during retirement is a recipe for disaster. It's what gave them joy, purpose and zest for living before they retired or (should I say) "attempted" to retire.

> *"If I am through learning, I am through."*
> -John Wooden, Legendary UCLA basketball coach

If this book has served as the catalyst, spark or as intended, an awakening for you at the right moment in time, then I am deeply honored and grateful. Many books, mentors, experiences and new found knowledge have positively impacted and enriched my own life. The classroom of life is always in session. Keep learning, pursuing, creating and pushing the realm of possibility. Life moves quickly. Each day is a massive blessing if you treat it as such. Others may fritter away their days, destiny, talents and valuable life force. Let your life be the exact opposite of this and serve as an inspiration and force for good.

I wish you Godspeed, happiness and massive success as you awaken, discover and build your own entrepreneurial genius!

# SECTION 3:

## MIND Maintenance – Additional Resources

# Additional FREE Resources

**FREE Bonus #1:**     **Audio Interviews with Tony and Two VIP Guests**

To receive the two free audio interviews with Dr. Ivan Misner and Jack Canfield simply visit:

**www.MindCaptureGroup.com/bonus.php**

**FREE Bonus #2:**     **Gift Account from SendOutCards and Mind Capture Group**

We'll let you send out two free greeting cards to see how powerful this relationship-building service is and why we use and promote it.

Send an email to Info@MindCaptureGroup.com with the Subject Line: "Book Offer for SOC" and a member of our team will be in touch with you.

**FREE Bonus #3:**     **Stay Connected to the Latest Updates by Joining us on Facebook**

**Simply visit: www.Facebook.com/trubleski**

In your friend request, please type the message: "Fan of book #3" so we can easily track how you heard about Tony and ensure that you're in fact a fan and are interested in sharing ideas.

# Additional Books to Engage
# & Awaken Your Mind

**Note:** Book titles are presented in no particular order. Each book contains valuable lessons and wisdom. There's an abundance of great knowledge to discover, engage and help shape your mind. Get busy!

* *How to Sell Your Way Through Life* by Napoleon Hill
* *No BS Wealth Attraction* by Dan Kennedy
* *The Success Principles* by Jack Canfield
* *Atlas Shrugged* and *The Fountainhead* by Ayn Rand
* *Think & Grow Rich* by Napoleon Hill
* *Three Feet from Gold* by Sharon Lechter and Greg Reid
* *Rich Dad Poor Dad* by Robert Kiyosaki and Sharon Lechter
* *The Presentation Secrets of Steve Jobs* by Carmine Gallo
* *Influence* by Robert Cialdini
* *The 29% Solution* by Ivan Misner and Michelle Pinney
* *Fahrenheit 451* by Ray Bradbury

- *Think Big & Kick Ass* by Donald Trump and Bill Zanker
- *Buying Trances* by Joe Vitale
- *Outrageous Advertising* by Bill Glazer
- *Me 2.0* by Dan Schawbel
- *The Science of getting Rich* by Wallace Wattles
- *The Secret* by Rhonda Byrne
- *Promptings* by Kody Bateman
- *Beach Money* by Jordan Adler
- *The Alchemist* by Paulo Coelho
- *The Sticking Point* by Jay Abraham
- *The Ultimate Sales Machine* by Chet Holmes
- *How to Master the Art of Selling* by Tom Hopkins
- *Win the Crowd* by Steve Cohen
- *The Collapse of Distinction* by Scott McKain
- *Failing Forward* by John Maxwell
- *The Last Lecture* by Randy Pausch and Jeff Zaslow
- *The Science of Influence* by Kevin Hogan
- *Sex Money Kiss* by Gene Simmons
- *The Breathing Blanket* by Greg Bauer
- *The Other 90%* by Robert Cooper
- *Never Fly Solo* by Rob Waldman
- *The True Believer* by Eric Hoffer
- *The Compound Effect* by Darren Hardy
- *The Tipping Point and Blink* by Malcolm Gladwell
- *Fearless and Reinventing Yourself* by Steve Chandler
- *Presentation Zen* by Garr Reynolds
- *The Go-Giver* by Bob Burg and John David Mann
- *You Were Born Rich* by Bob Proctor

- *The First Billion is the Hardest* by T. Boone Pickens
- *Beyond Doubt* by John Murphy
- *Winning in Life Now* by Michelle Prince
- *The Referral of a Lifetime* by Tim Templeton
- *The Referral Engine* by John Jantsch
- *Street Smart Persuasion* by Mike Dolphies
- *Texas in Her Own Words* by Tweed Scott
- *Eat that Frog* by Brian Tracy
- *Trump Style Negotiation* by George Ross
- *Powerlines* by Steve Cone
- *The Secret Code of Success* by Noah St. John
- *The Yellow Book of Yes* and *The Little Red Book of Selling* by Jeffrey Gitomer
- *The Little Red Book of Wisdom* by Mark DeMoss
- *Click Here to Order and KaChing* by Joel Comm
- *The World is Flat* by Thomas Friedman
- *We Got Fired* by Harvey Mackay
- *The On-Purpose Person* by Kevin McCarthy
- *Wikinomics* by Don Tapscott
- *Read for Your Life* by Pat Williams
- *Speedwealth* by T. Harv Eker
- *FREE and The Long Tail* by Christopher Anderson
- *Bank on Yourself* by Pamela Yellen
- *The Grateful Dad* by John Trayser
- *A Whole New Mind* by Daniel Pink
- *Linchpin* by Seth Godin
- *The Shack* by WM Paul Young
- *eBoot Camp* by Corey Perlman

- *Six Pixels of Separation* by Mitch Joel
- *Action* by Robert Ringer
- *Uncensored Sales Strategies* by Sidney Barrows and Dan Kennedy
- *People are Idiots & I Can Prove it* by Larry Wingett
- *Always Looking Up* by Michael J. Fox
- *Author & Get Rich* by Glenn Dietzel
- *Creating Your Own Destiny* by Patrick Snow
- *The Power of the Platform* by Robin Jay
- *Liquid Leadership* by Brad Szollose
- *The Answer* by John Assaraf and Murray Smith
- *Find Your Why & Fly* by John DiLemme
- *No Excuses* by Kyle Maynard
- *Arnold: The Education of a Bodybuilder* by Arnold Schwarzenegger
- *Time Traps* by Todd Duncan
- *Pursuit* by Dexter Yager and John Mason
- *Crossing the Chasm* by Geoffrey Moore
- *Confessions of an SOB* by Al Neuharth
- *1776* by David McCullough
- *90 Minutes in Heaven* by Don Piper
- *Instant Income* by Janet Switzer
- *5 Cool Ideas for Better Working, Living & Feeling* by Michael Angelo Caruso
- *The Starbucks Experience* by Joseph Michelli
- *Move On: Your Life is Waiting* by Johnny Campbell
- *10 Steps to Financial Wellness* by Jeff Rubleski
- *Go for No* by Richard Fenton and Andrea Waltz
- *Younger Next Year* by Chris Crowley and Henry Lodge
- *The Power of Now* by Eckhart Tolle